Introducing Artificial Intelligence: A Beginner's Guide

Somayeh Babaei Tarkami

Ali Mohammadiounotikandi

Title: Artificial Intelligence Introduction: A Beginner's Guide

Author: Somayeh Babaei Tarkami, Ali Mohammadiounotikandi

Cover Designer: Somayeh Babaei Tarkami

Publisher: American Academic Research, USA

ISBN: 9781947464407

Contents

About the authors

Somayeh Babaei Tarkami is an Iranian-Turkish author and graphic designer, born in 1983 in Iran. With a passion for art and design from a young age, Somayeh pursued a career in graphic design and obtained a Master's degree in the field. She has over 15 years of experience in advertising and sales management and more than 8 years of research activity in the IT industry and information security management.

Somayeh is also an IT security consultant, with certifications in ISO and PMP, demonstrating her commitment to staying up-to-date with the latest developments in the field. As the founder of Bahman Information Processing Company, she holds DBA certificates, ISO 9001 and ISO 27001.

In addition to her work in design and security, Somayeh is an accomplished writer with several published works exploring topics such as design, creativity, and entrepreneurship. Her writing draws on her own experiences as a designer and consultant, offering insights and advice to aspiring creatives and entrepreneurs.

Somayeh is an active member of the creative community in Iran and beyond, participating in exhibitions, conferences, and workshops to share her knowledge and expertise. Her work has earned her a reputation as a leading voice in the fields of design and security, and she continues to inspire others with her creativity and insight.

Ali Mohammadiounotikandi is an Iranian-Turkish author and IT professional born in 1986 in Iran. Growing up in Iran, Ali developed an interest in literature and technology at an early age, leading him to pursue a career in the IT field while also exploring his passion for writing.

After completing his education in computer science and obtaining a Master's degree in IT, Ali began working in the IT industry, gaining expertise in areas such as software development, network engineering, and information security. He has earned several professional certifications, including CompTIA, Microsoft, Linux, ISACA, and ISO 27001 and 9001, demonstrating his commitment to staying up-to-date with the latest developments in the field.

He has also authored several articles in respected academic journals, earning recognition from the ISI and Scopus indices.

The title "Security Reference in Computer Networks Based on the Topics of Security+" has been selected as one of the references for the Ph.D. entrance exam of Information Technology Engineering, 2022, Iran.

The title "Network+ from 0 to 100" has been chosen as the selected book of the Agriculture Bank for teaching and research purposes, 2022, Iran.

Achieved the first stage of the National Students Mathematics Olympiad, 2002, Iran.

Some several books and ideas have been published in the United States before that.

To our beloved son Bardia, this book is dedicated to you. *As we worked together on this project, we were constantly reminded of the importance of family, and how our loved ones can inspire and support us in all that we do. You have been a constant source of joy and inspiration in our lives, and it is with gratitude and love that we dedicate this book to you. Through your boundless curiosity, your infectious enthusiasm, and your unwavering support, you have taught us the power of collaboration, and the importance of pursuing our dreams with passion and purpose. We hope that one day you will read these pages and see a reflection of yourself in them and that you will feel a sense of pride in the knowledge that you played a vital role in bringing this book to life. May this book serve as a testament to the power of family to inspire and uplift us in all that we do and as a reminder of the unbreakable bond that we share as a family.* ***We love you, Bardia****.*

Introduction

Somayeh and Ali sat across from each other, their laptops open in front of them. They had been working on their book for months, and the deadline was quickly approaching. The topic was complex, and they needed to make sure their arguments were clear and concise. Ali leaned forward and asked, "What if we started the chapter with a real-life example of how AI is being used in healthcare?" Somayeh nodded, "That's a great idea. We could talk about how AI is helping doctors diagnose diseases faster and more accurately." They began to write, each taking turns to add their perspectives and insights. As they worked, they found themselves challenging each other's assumptions and ideas, pushing themselves to create a more compelling argument. They took breaks to discuss their progress and share their frustrations, but always came back to the task at hand. Finally, they finished the chapter, feeling a sense of accomplishment that they had worked together to create something meaningful and informative. They looked at each other and smiled, knowing that their book had the potential to change the way people think about AI and its impact on healthcare.

Introduction to artificial intelligence

Artificial intelligence, or AI, is a branch of computer science concerned with creating computer systems capable of performing tasks that normally require human intelligence. Perception, reasoning, decision-making, and natural language understanding are examples of these tasks.

Artificial intelligence is frequently divided into two categories: narrow or weak AI and general or strong AI. Narrow AI refers to systems that are designed to perform a single task, such as facial or speech recognition. In contrast, general AI refers to systems that can perform any intellectual task that a human can.

Since its inception in the 1950s, artificial intelligence has come a long way. AI is now used in a wide variety of applications, from virtual assistants like Siri and Alexa to self-driving cars, medical diagnosis, and even art and music creation.

Despite the numerous benefits of AI, there are concerns about its impact on society. Some are concerned that AI will result in job loss and income inequality, while others are concerned about the ethical implications of using AI in fields such as warfare or law enforcement.

AI has the potential to transform how we live and work. As AI advances, it is critical that we consider both its benefits and potential risks, and that it is developed and used responsibly and ethically.

Artificial intelligence (AI) has the potential to benefit a wide range of fields and industries. Here are a few of the potential advantages of AI:

Increased productivity and efficiency

I can automate time-consuming and repetitive tasks, freeing up human workers to focus on more complex and creative tasks.

Improved accuracy and precision

AI can perform tasks with high accuracy and precision, lowering the possibility of errors and improving overall quality.

Enhanced decision-making

AI can analyze massive amounts of data and provide insights and recommendations to help people make better decisions.

Cost savings

AI can help organizations reduce costs and save money by automating tasks and increasing efficiency.

Personalization

Individuals' experiences can be personalized using AI, such as recommending products or services based on their preferences and past behavior.

Improved healthcare

AI can be used to analyze medical data and assist healthcare providers in developing more accurate diagnoses and treatment plans.

Enhanced safety and security

Artificial intelligence (AI) can be used to monitor and detect potential threats such as cyber-attacks or physical security breaches.

Advancements in scientific research

Artificial intelligence (AI) can be used to analyze complex scientific data and accelerate research in fields such as astronomy, genetics, and physics.

AI has the potential to provide numerous benefits to society while also revolutionizing how we live and work. However, as AI advances, it is critical to consider the potential risks and ethical implications.

While Artificial Intelligence (AI) has many potential benefits, there are also concerns about the risks it may pose.

Some of the potential dangers of AI:

Job displacement

As AI and automation advance, there is a risk that machines will replace many jobs, resulting in unemployment and income inequality.

Bias and discrimination

AI systems can only be as objective as the data on which they are trained. If the underlying data is biased, the resulting AI system may perpetuate bias and discrimination.

Privacy concerns

AI systems frequently collect and analyze large amounts of personal data, raising privacy and data protection concerns.

Autonomous weapons

There is a risk that AI-powered autonomous weapons will cause unintentional harm and loss of human life if they malfunction or are used maliciously.

Cybersecurity risks

AI systems are susceptible to cyber-attacks and hacking, which could result in data breaches or other security breaches.

Lack of accountability

As AI systems become more complex, determining who is accountable for their actions and decisions can become difficult, raising concerns about accountability and transparency.

Existential risks

There is a theoretical risk that AI systems will become super intelligent and endanger humanity.

As AI advances, it is critical to carefully consider the potential dangers and take steps to mitigate these risks, and ensure that AI is developed and used responsibly and ethically.

The history of Artificial Intelligence

The origins of Artificial Intelligence (AI) can be traced back to the mid-twentieth century when researchers began to investigate the possibility of creating machines that could think and reason like humans.

Here's a quick rundown of AI's history:

The birth of AI

Artificial intelligence (AI) has its origins in the mid-twentieth century when researchers began to investigate the possibility of creating machines capable of thinking and reasoning like humans. Here's a primer on artificial intelligence:

The early years

Researchers made significant progress in developing AI algorithms and techniques in the years following the Dartmouth Conference. Early breakthroughs included the creation of the first AI programs capable of playing games such as checkers and chess.

The rise of expert systems

There was a shift in the 1970s and 1980s toward developing expert systems - AI programs that could mimic the decision-making abilities of human experts in specific domains.

The AI winters

AI progress slowed in the late 1980s and early 1990s, and funding for AI research dried up. The "AI winter" was caused by a combination of factors, including overhype and unrealistic expectations.

The resurgence of AI

AI progress began to accelerate again in the 2000s, thanks to advances in machine learning and the availability of large datasets. Among the technological advances made during this period were the development of self-driving cars and the creation of intelligent virtual assistants such as Siri and Alexa.

The current state of AI

Today, artificial intelligence is an active and rapidly evolving field, with researchers and developers experimenting with new applications and techniques. Deep learning, natural language processing, and robotics are three of the most exciting areas of AI research today.

AI's history is marked by periods of rapid advancement and excitement, followed by periods of disappointment and stagnation. Despite these obstacles, AI has continued to advance, and it is now poised to revolutionize many aspects of our lives.

AI breakthrough allows computers to learn like humans

Artificial intelligence (AI) breakthroughs have enabled computers to learn in the same way that humans do, a field of AI research known as "machine learning." Machine learning refers to computers' ability to learn and improve based on experience without being explicitly programmed to do so.

A human programmer writes code that instructs the computer on how to perform a specific task in traditional programming. In machine learning, on the other hand, the computer is fed data and trained to recognize patterns and make predictions based on that data. This is similar to how humans learn: by observing and connecting disparate pieces of information.

The redevelopment of neural networks is one of the key breakthroughs that have enabled computers to learn like humans. Neural networks are computer systems that are structured like the human brain, with layers of interconnected nodes that process data. These networks can learn and adapt to new information in the same way that humans can.

The development of deep learning algorithms is another machine learning breakthrough. These algorithms can quickly and accurately process and analyze large amounts of data, making them useful in a variety of applications ranging from image and speech recognition to natural language processing.

With these AI advances, computers can now learn from experience and make decisions in much the same way that humans do. This has resulted in many exciting advances in fields like healthcare, finance, and transportation, as well as advancements in consumer technology like virtual assistants and smart home devices.

How AI is revolutionizing healthcare

Five novel applications

AI is transforming healthcare by increasing the accuracy and speed of medical diagnoses, assisting in drug discovery, and optimizing treatment plans. Here are five creative applications of artificial intelligence in healthcare:

Medical imaging

AI can analyze medical images such as X-rays and MRIs to detect potential abnormalities that would otherwise go undetected. Machine learning algorithms can learn to recognize patterns in medical images that could indicate a specific disease or condition.

Artificial intelligence (AI) is transforming medical imaging as one of the ways it is revolutionizing healthcare. Medical imaging is an important tool in diagnosing and treating a wide range of conditions, and AI is making it faster and more accurate than ever before.

Here is some ways AI is revolutionizing medical imaging:

Improved accuracy

AI algorithms can analyze medical images such as X-rays, CT scans, and MRIs to detect subtle changes that the human eye may miss. This can lead to more accurate diagnoses and earlier disease detection.

Faster diagnoses

AI can quickly process large volumes of medical images, reducing the time required to diagnose and treat patients. This is especially important in situations where time is of the essence.

Reduced costs

By automating the analysis of medical images, AI can help reduce healthcare costs. This allows healthcare providers to focus on patient care while reducing the need for costly imaging equipment and specialized knowledge.

Personalized treatment

Based on the unique characteristics of each patient's medical images, AI can assist healthcare providers in developing personalized treatment plans. This may result in more effective treatments and improved patient outcomes.

Remote diagnosis

AI-powered medical imaging can be used to remotely diagnose patients, which is particularly useful in rural or underserved areas where access to medical specialists may be limited. This has the potential to improve patient outcomes by allowing for faster access to critical diagnostic information.

Finally, AI is transforming medical imaging, which is revolutionizing healthcare. AI-powered medical imaging is increasing diagnostic accuracy and speed, lowering costs, and enabling personalized treatment plans. As AI technology advances, it will almost certainly play a larger role in the diagnosis and treatment of many diseases.

Predictive analytics

Large amounts of patient data can be analyzed by AI to identify patterns and predict future health outcomes. This can assist healthcare providers in identifying patients at high risk of developing certain conditions and intervening sooner to prevent disease progression.

AI is transforming healthcare by enabling predictive analytics, which involves analyzing large amounts of patient data to identify patterns and predict future health outcomes. Here are some examples of how artificial intelligence (AI) is transforming healthcare through predictive analytics:

Early detection is critical.

AI algorithms can analyze patient data such as medical history, lifestyle factors, and genetic information to identify patients who are predisposed to certain diseases. This allows doctors to intervene early and prevent disease progression.

Precision medicine

Based on a patient's unique health data, AI can assist healthcare providers in developing personalized treatment plans. This has the potential to result in more effective treatments and better patient outcomes.

Resource distribution

AI can help healthcare providers allocate resources more efficiently by predicting which patients are most likely to require hospitalization or other forms of medical intervention. This can help to reduce healthcare costs while also improving patient care.

Clinical trial optimization

AI can assist pharmaceutical companies in optimizing clinical trials by identifying patients who are most likely to respond to a specific treatment. This can help bring new treatments to market more quickly and affordably.

Public health monitoring

AI can analyze large amounts of data from social media, news sources, and other online sources to identify emerging health threats like infectious disease outbreaks. This allows public health officials to respond quickly and effectively to public health threats.

AI is transforming healthcare by enabling predictive analytics, which can improve patient outcomes, lower healthcare costs, and accelerate medical research. As AI technology advances, it will almost certainly play a larger role in the prevention, diagnosis, and treatment of many diseases.

Personalized treatment plans

AI can analyze patient data to assist healthcare providers in developing personalized treatment plans that are tailored to the specific needs of each individual. Avoiding unnecessary treatments can help improve patient outcomes while also lowering healthcare costs.

Drug discovery

By identifying promising compounds and predicting their efficacy in clinical trials, AI can help pharmaceutical companies accelerate the drug discovery process. This can help bring new treatments to market more quickly and affordably.

Artificial intelligence (AI) is transforming the drug discovery process, which is revolutionizing healthcare. By identifying promising compounds and predicting their efficacy in clinical trials, AI is assisting pharmaceutical companies in accelerating drug discovery. Here are some examples of how AI is transforming drug discovery:

Accelerated drug discovery

To identify promising drug candidates, AI can analyze massive amounts of data from scientific literature, clinical trials, and other sources. This can speed up drug discovery by allowing researchers to focus on the most promising compounds.

Reduced costs

AI can help reduce drug development costs by allowing researchers to identify promising drug candidates more quickly and accurately. This can help bring new treatments to market more quickly and affordably.

Improved success rates

AI can help pharmaceutical companies identify which drugs are most likely to succeed in the market by predicting the efficacy of drug candidates in clinical trials. This can increase clinical trial success rates while decreasing the risk of costly failures.

Personalized medicine

AI can assist in identifying patient subgroups that are more likely to respond to a specific treatment. This can help pharmaceutical companies develop personalized treatments that are tailored to the specific needs of each patient.

Drug repurposing

AI can assist in the identification of existing drugs that could be repurposed to treat other diseases. This can hasten the development of new treatments by utilizing existing drugs that have already been approved for human use.

AI is transforming the drug discovery process, which is revolutionizing healthcare. AI-powered drug discovery is hastening the development of new treatments while lowering costs and increasing success rates. As AI technology advances, it will almost certainly play a larger role in the development of new treatments for a wide range of diseases.

Virtual assistants

Chatbots and voice assistants powered by AI can help patients manage their healthcare needs by providing personalized advice and guidance. These virtual assistants can make it easier for patients to schedule appointments, refill prescriptions, and access medical information.

AI has the potential to transform healthcare by improving diagnosis accuracy and speed, assisting in drug discovery, and optimizing treatment plans. These novel applications are just a few examples of how artificial intelligence is transforming the healthcare industry and improving patient outcomes.

AI is transforming healthcare by enabling the development of virtual assistants, also known as chatbots or conversational agents. Virtual assistants are computer programs that can communicate with patients and healthcare providers to provide information, answer questions, and even provide basic medical advice. Here are some examples of how artificial intelligence is transforming healthcare through virtual assistants:

Improved patient engagement

Patients can benefit from personalized, interactive support from virtual assistants to help them manage their health more effectively. This can increase patient engagement and help patients make better health decisions.

Increased efficiency

Virtual assistants can help healthcare providers save time and money by automating routine tasks like appointment scheduling and prescription refills.

Better access to care

Virtual assistants can provide patients with access to basic medical information and advice 24 hours a day, seven days a week, which is especially beneficial for patients who live in rural or underserved areas.

Personalized medicine

AI can be used by virtual assistants to analyze patient data and make personalized treatment recommendations based on each patient's unique health profile.

Improved patient outcomes

Virtual assistants can track patient symptoms and provide real-time feedback, assisting healthcare providers in identifying potential issues before they become serious. This can result in better patient outcomes and fewer hospitalizations.

AI is transforming healthcare by enabling the development of virtual assistants that can provide personalized, interactive support to patients. Virtual assistants can help improve patient engagement, efficiency, and access to care. As AI technology advances, virtual assistants will likely play a larger role in the delivery of healthcare services.

The ethical implications of AI

Artificial intelligence (AI) is rapidly changing our world and has the potential to provide significant societal benefits. However, it raises several ethical concerns and challenges that we must consider.

Here are some of the ethical implications of AI that we must consider:

Bias and discrimination

AI systems are prone to bias, which often reflects the biases of their designers or the data on which they are trained. This may result in discrimination against specific groups of people. It is critical to ensure that artificial intelligence systems are designed to be fair and unbiased, and that they do not perpetuate existing social inequalities.

The potential for AI systems to perpetuate or even amplify existing biases and inequalities in society is referred to as bias and discrimination in AI. AI systems are frequently trained on large datasets, which can contain implicit biases that are reflected in the system's algorithms. As a result, certain groups of people, such as minorities, women, and people with disabilities, may face discrimination.

For example, it has been demonstrated that facial recognition algorithms have higher error rates for women and people of color, which can lead to discriminatory outcomes in areas such as law enforcement or hiring practices. Language models trained on biased datasets, on the other hand, can perpetuate stereotypes and reinforce discriminatory attitudes.

Bias and discrimination in AI have significant ethical implications because they can result in unfair treatment and harm to individuals and groups. AI systems must be designed to be fair and unbiased, and they must be audited regularly to identify and correct any biases that may exist. This can include things like using different datasets and involving a variety of stakeholders in the design process, as well as testing and monitoring the system for bias regularly.

Privacy and surveillance

AI systems can collect massive amounts of data about individuals, which can then be used for surveillance and monitoring. This raises privacy concerns as well as the possibility of data misuse.

Because AI systems can collect and process vast amounts of personal data, privacy, and surveillance are important ethical implications of AI. This information can be used to monitor and track people, often without their knowledge or consent, raising serious privacy concerns.

AI systems, such as facial recognition technology used by law enforcement agencies, can also be used for surveillance. This can raise concerns about civil liberties and the potential for this technology to be abused.

Because AI systems can be used to collect and process personal data for targeted advertising, the use of AI in advertising and marketing can also raise privacy concerns. This raises concerns about the manipulation of people's choices and behaviors.

AI systems must be designed with privacy in mind, and individuals must have control over how their data is collected, processed, and used. Clear and transparent data policies, user consent for data collection and processing, and secure data storage and transfer are examples of such measures. Furthermore, regulations and standards to govern the use of AI in areas such as surveillance and advertising can be established to ensure that it is used in ways that protect individual privacy rights.

Autonomous decision-making

As AI systems advance in sophistication, they will increasingly make decisions on their own, without the need for human intervention. This begs the question of who is accountable for the decisions made by these systems and how we can ensure that they are ethical and in line with human values.

Another significant ethical implication of AI is autonomous decision-making. As AI systems advance in sophistication, they may be able to make decisions autonomously, without the need for human intervention. This begs the question of who is accountable for the decisions made by these systems and how we can ensure that they are ethical and in line with human values.

Autonomous vehicles, for example, can make decisions about how to navigate traffic or avoid accidents, raising questions about who is liable for any accidents that occur. Similarly, AI systems used in finance or healthcare can make loan or medical treatment decisions that have serious consequences for individuals.

To address these concerns, clear guidelines and ethical principles for the use of AI in decision-making must be established. Establishing decision-making criteria such as transparency, fairness, and accountability, and ensuring that these criteria are integrated into the design and implementation of AI systems, can be part of this.

Furthermore, regulations and standards may be required to ensure that AI is used in ways that are consistent with human values and ethics and that any negative consequences are mitigated. Finally, AI systems may require ongoing monitoring and evaluation to ensure that they are operating ethically and by human values.

Job displacement

Many jobs could be automated by AI, resulting in significant job displacement and social upheaval. It is critical to consider how we can mitigate the negative effects of artificial intelligence on employment and ensure that people can adapt to new job markets.

Another significant ethical implication of AI is job displacement. As AI systems advance, they have the potential to automate many tasks that are currently performed by humans, potentially displacing workers in a variety of industries.

This can have serious economic and social consequences, as workers may struggle to find new jobs and may face financial hardship as a result of losing their jobs. Furthermore, worker displacement can lead to income and wealth inequalities, as those who can benefit from the use of AI may see significant gains, while others may struggle to find new employment.

To address these concerns, it is critical to ensure that the benefits of artificial intelligence are distributed fairly and equitably. This can include measures such as retraining programs to assist workers in developing the skills required for new jobs, as well as social safety nets to assist those who are unable to find work. Furthermore, policies and regulations to ensure that the benefits of AI are shared more broadly, such as through taxes or other mechanisms, may be required.

It is also critical to consider the long-term impact of AI on employment and the economy, as well as to investigate new work and employment models that may emerge as a result of AI. This can include investigating the possibility of new job types or greater flexibility in work arrangements. Finally, the goal should be to ensure that the benefits of AI are fairly distributed and that its use does not result in increased inequality or hardship for workers.

Safety and Security

AI systems can become more dangerous as they become more powerful if they are not designed with safety and security in mind. This includes the possibility of AI being used in cyberattacks or causing physical harm.

Accountability: As AI systems become more autonomous, it becomes more difficult to assign blame for their actions. It is critical to establish clear lines of accountability and hold those in charge of AI systems accountable for their actions.

Because AI systems can have serious consequences if they malfunction or are used maliciously, safety and security are important ethical implications of AI. Individuals may be physically harmed, property may be damaged, or critical systems and infrastructure may be disrupted.

Autonomous vehicles, for example, can pose a safety risk if they malfunction or are hacked, potentially resulting in accidents or other harm to individuals. Similarly, AI systems used in critical infrastructure, such as power or water systems, can be vulnerable to cyberattacks or other forms of malicious activity, causing significant disruptions and harm.

To address these concerns, AI systems must be designed with safety and security in mind, with appropriate safeguards and controls in place to prevent harm. This can include rigorous testing and validation of AI systems, the use of encryption and other data security measures, and the establishment of standards and regulations to ensure that AI is used in safe and secure ways.

Furthermore, ongoing monitoring and evaluation of AI systems may be required to ensure that they are operating safely and securely, as well as to identify and address any potential risks or vulnerabilities. This may necessitate collaboration among stakeholders from various industries and sectors, as well as ongoing research and development to improve AI system safety and security. Finally, the goal should be to use AI in ways that are safe, secure, and consistent with human values and ethics.

Transparency

It can be difficult to understand how AI systems make decisions, making it difficult to hold them accountable. It is critical that AI systems are transparent and that people understand how they make decisions.

Transparency is an important ethical implication of AI because it can help to ensure that AI systems are accountable and that humans can understand and evaluate their decisions and actions. In AI systems, a lack of transparency can raise concerns about bias, discrimination, and the potential for harm.

To address these concerns, AI systems must be designed with transparency in mind, and appropriate mechanisms must be in place to allow for human oversight and understanding of AI system decisions. Clear and transparent data policies, explanations of how AI systems make decisions, and the ability for humans to intervene in the decision-making process if necessary are examples of such measures.

Furthermore, regulations and standards may be required to ensure that AI systems are transparent and accountable and that they are used in ways that are consistent with human values and ethics. This may necessitate collaboration among stakeholders from various industries and sectors, as well as ongoing research and development to improve AI system transparency and accountability.

Finally, the goal should be to ensure that artificial intelligence is used in ways that are transparent, accountable, and consistent with human values and ethics.

We can help to build trust in AI systems and ensure that they are used in ways that benefit society as a whole by promoting transparency.

AI-powered robots could soon take over dangerous jobs

People have been debating the impact of artificial intelligence and other new automated technology on America's job market since ChatGPT took the world by storm last fall. The narrative that "robots are taking our jobs" was bolstered further by viral videos showing new, "fully automated" McDonald's and Taco Bell locations.

The immediate reaction to these videos is to fear that robots will take our jobs; however, while AI and other forms of automation have advanced, this does not necessarily imply that they will eliminate jobs. Instead, new technology is simply altering how we work and the types of jobs that exist. Behind screens, machines, and smiling robot faces, automation technology has ushered in a fleet of secret workers. Robots and chatbots do not replace humans; they simply keep them out of sight and out of mind. While separating customers from the employees who serve them may benefit the companies, there is mounting evidence that it is a bad deal for the employees.

Out of sight, out of mind

When people predict that AI will take our jobs, they like to show videos of sleek robots and gleaming screens performing mundane tasks. The McDonald's video depicts a machine delivering food at the drive-thru, self-ordering kiosks, and a distinct lack of human employees behind the order counter. There are several automated drive-thru lanes at Taco Bell. Aside from fast food, impressive-looking robots are delivering food and cleaning floors in coffee shops. On the AI front, ChatGPT tools have been used to write real articles and take college exams. BuzzFeed recently announced plans to use artificial intelligence to help generate content for its website.

However, in many cases, these videos and stories — and the fears they inspire — are devoid of critical context. The futuristic McDonald's is a concept store outside of Fort Worth, Texas, that aims to improve service speed and accuracy by effectively severing the relationship between its employees and customers. However, this does not imply that there are no humans in the store. If you watch the video closely, you can see a worker in the back behind a pane of glass. McDonald's has stated that the store is not "fully automated," and that it employs a comparable number of employees to a traditional store — they're just in the back making the food and keeping things running.

And, while most customers will never see a Taco Bell employee at its newfangled location, there are plenty of people working in the kitchen.

Even though these tools appear to be more sophisticated, this isn't the first time a robot-driven freak-out has occurred. Less than a decade ago, new technological developments sparked a similar fear that robots were on their way to us. According to a 2014 study, automation will eliminate 47% of all jobs by 2034, and self-driving technology will eliminate the need for human taxi and delivery drivers, while long-haul truckers are on borrowed time.

These cataclysmic predictions have yet to come true nearly a decade later. Truck drivers remain in high demand, and self-driving technology is far from replacing human jobs. According to a more recent World Economic Forum 2020 report, while machines are expected to replace 85 million jobs by 2025, an estimated 97 million new jobs will be created to support this new economy.

The human behind the curtain

People frequently overlook the extent to which machines still require human workers to function amid the fear-mongering about a robot takeover. Consider customer service: Businesses have been attempting to cut costs for years by replacing human phone calls with chat-based, automated customer service bots. However, rather than replacing customer service representatives, many of these text-based tools still rely on human backups in complex situations to give customers the impression that they are speaking with a real person.

Laura Preston recently wrote about her experience as one of these "human fallbacks" for Brenda, a real-estate chatbot. When a customer called about an apartment listing, they were connected with Brenda, who could answer basic questions about the listing or provide details on the apartment itself, such as the rent and square footage. However, many of Brenda's responses were stilted, or the system was simply unable to answer more complex questions, so a "human fallback" would be invoked. Preston and other human workers would take over the conversation and attempt to assist the client, cleaning up stock answers to better address their needs or conducting more in-depth research into housing vouchers and pet policies.

Preston claims that employees were trained to use Brenda's "voice" in interactions to make the conversation appear seamless. The pressure to answer questions robotically took a mental toll: "Months of impersonating Brenda had depleted my emotional resources," Preston wrote. "I realized I wasn't training Brenda to think like a human, but rather Brenda was training me to think like a bot, and perhaps that was the point all along."

Preston was working from the United States, but in many cases, these services conceal human employees to outsource to places where labor is less expensive. Consider food-delivery robots:

While they are presented as fully autonomous, they frequently have remote backup drivers. Tiny Mile, which operates the Geoffrey service in Toronto, uses drivers from the Philippines, while Kiwi's robots, which are used on some US college campuses, have been known to use workers from Colombia earning less than $2 per hour to help complete deliveries. Companies claim that remote drivers only take over when the robots are unable to navigate a situation, but given how prone these robots are to becoming stuck and becoming obstacles for sidewalk users, it's unclear how frequently this occurs.

Many of the leading companies developing self-driving vehicles, which have threatened to replace a wide range of driving jobs in the future, also rely on a fleet of unnoticed workers. There are highly-paid engineers in the United States who contribute to the development of the software and tools used to map and guide the car, but that isn't the whole picture. Autonomous driving technology is reliant on low-wage workers all over the world who label the thousands of data inputs captured by the car's sensors.

Without that labeling, the computer would be unable to identify what the sensors are sensing, allowing the systems to gradually learn and make decisions about how to navigate the road. For example, data labeling is supposed to assist cars in determining whether an obstruction is a child or a traffic cone — but it doesn't always work as planned. An MIT Technology Review investigation last April discovered that self-driving companies, including Tesla, took advantage of Venezuela's economic collapse by hiring workers in the country to label self-driving data for just over 90 cents an hour.

Tesla laid off 200 US-based workers it directly employed to do this labeling last year, implying that it was instead automating the majority of those tasks

a computer teaching another computer.

It isn't just self-driving technology. According to a recent Time magazine investigation, Open AI, the company behind ChatGPT, relies on Kenyan workers paid less than $2 per hour to view content on a variety of disturbing topics.

Including "child sexual abuse, bestiality, murder, suicide, torture, self-harm, and incest" in an attempt to make the tool less toxic. This is in addition to an earlier report claiming that Facebook uses the same subcontractor in Kenya for its content moderation. Other companies have gone so far as to recruit workers in refugee camps, where opportunities are scarce and people are willing to accept extremely low wages, to assist in the training of their machine learning and AI tools. Far from being "set it and forget it" tools that require only a few genius coders, many of these ostensibly autonomous marvels rely on a global army of low-paid workers.

The myth of efficiency

Companies will tell you that the automation push is all about efficiency and better-serving customers. McDonald's claims that its concept store will improve service and result in fewer incorrect orders, whereas Tesla claims that automating data labeling is more efficient. The idea is that these machines or software solutions will make a job faster or better, making life easier for businesses and customers alike. However, these tools do not make the process more efficient; they simply shift the necessary work away from the end user and disconnect people from the effort required to deliver a product.

For one thing, it's unclear whether all of the newfangled tools developed by businesses are making the economy more efficient. Since 2005, the United States labor productivity — the number of worker hours required to produce a given amount of economic output — has been growing at a rate lower than its long-run average. Despite hopes that the forced digital transition would help, productivity growth has only gotten worse since the pandemic began.

Instead of increasing productivity, automation is frequently used to increase employers' power over workers. In his book, "Automation and the Future of Work," economic historian Aaron Benanav explains that companies are investing in "technologies allowing for detailed surveillance of those same workers," such as computer-monitoring software that tracks employees' keystrokes or Amazon's sophisticated algorithmic management tools that evaluate workers' every movement.

These technologies are frequently used to de-skill work, which means that jobs are broken down into more specific tasks that can be completed with less training. As a result, workers' status is changed from employee to contractor. People who used to work in stable, middle-class jobs are now thrown into a more precarious world where wages are lower and they have less say over their working conditions. Data labelers are just the tip of the iceberg:

A large (and growing) industry of "micro workers" on platforms like Mechanical Turk or Click worker fuels all of these tech companies' ostensibly automated tech. Amazon CEO Jeff Bezos has gone so far as to refer to the use of workers to make a process appear automated as "artificial intelligence." For those who still work in service or warehouse jobs, the threat of automation is wielded like a Sword of Damocles, preventing them from advocating for better working conditions or wages.

Meanwhile, the deployed technologies simply give employers more power to track everything workers do while on the clock — a depressing working reality. In 2015, journalist Lauren Smiley wrote that this trend was creating a world in which "you're either pampered, isolated royalty — or a 21st-century servant."

There is no doubt that some of these technologies provide consumers with conveniences or even free up their time so they can focus on their work, but this does not excuse the treatment of the workers on whom they rely. The technology could be used to empower workers, for example, by giving them more control over their work so they can use their skills to make more informed decisions, but companies frequently do not share that data.

Instead of using new technology for good, Phil Jones, a researcher, and author of "Work Without the

Worker: Laboure in the Age of Platform Capitalism," contends that companies use semi-automated technology to make it appear as if executives or the brand itself deserve all of the credit for the end product, rather than the human employees who made it possible. "Workers vanish in the long shadow of the machine," Jones writes, and customers and clients are less concerned about how the sausage is made. Meanwhile, job quality is deteriorating.

AI is framed as providing various forms of empowerment and liberation: we will be able to work more productively, spend less time doing chores, and everything we want will be a click or tap away. However, those promises never paint an accurate picture of how that technology is transforming our world or the true cost of those ostensible benefits. Automation may empower some people, but it makes life much more difficult for unseen workers who keep everything running.

Is AI the key to unlocking sustainable energy solutions?

The energy sector faces pressing challenges and must act quickly. Policy commitments to a net-zero future, such as the Paris Agreement, require a rapid transition to a low-carbon economy.

As governments ramp up renewables and transition away from fossil fuels, the electricity sector will face significant disruption. While renewable energy appears to be thriving in this environment, its intermittent nature necessitates the development of solutions to keep grids stable. Furthermore, to integrate renewable energy, the industry is transitioning from a market based on commodity pricing to a market based on technology solutions. As the energy industry uses more variable generation sources, accurate forecasts of power generation and netload are becoming increasingly important for maintaining system reliability, reducing carbon emissions, and maximizing renewable energy resources.

As we enter the Fourth Industrial Revolution, grid operators, developers, and consumers are embracing artificial intelligence (AI), paving the way for a more seamless transition to greater use of renewables. The ability of AI to provide better prediction capabilities enables improved demand forecasting and asset management, while its automation capability drives operational excellence, resulting in competitive advantage and cost savings for stakeholders.

AI has the potential to unlock the vast potential of renewables when combined with other emerging technologies such as the internet of things (IoT), sensors, big data, and distributed ledger technology. If it is not adopted, the renewable energy sector will fall behind.

When it comes to performing complex tasks quickly, AI far outperforms humans. Given that an energy grid is one of the most complex machines ever built, and that split-second decisions must be made in real-time, AI algorithms are an ideal fit.

How AI is transforming renewable energy

From demand forecasting to asset maintenance, the use of AI could yield benefits on multiple fronts.

As more megawatts are fed into the grid from variable renewable energy sources, predicting capacity levels has become critical to ensuring a stable and efficient grid. This is because, as renewables take a larger share of the grid, there is a loss of baseload generation from sources like coal, which provide grid inertia through the presence of heavy rotating equipment like steam and gas turbines.

Power networks will be unstable and prone to blackouts if grid inertia is not present. Solar and wind generation can now provide enormous amounts of real-time data, allowing AI to predict capacity levels, thanks to the use of sensor technology.

Before the use of AI, most forecasting techniques relied on individual weather models, which provided a limited view of the variables that affect renewable energy availability. AI programs, such as IBM's program for the US Department of Energy's SunShot Initiative, have now been developed that combine self-learning weather models, datasets of historical weather data, the real-time measurement from local weather stations, sensor networks, and cloud information derived from satellite imagery and sky cameras.

As a result, solar forecasting accuracy has improved by 30%, resulting in gains on multiple fronts. "We discovered that improved solar forecasts reduced operational electricity generation costs, the conventional generator starts and shutdown costs, and solar power curtailment," says Hendrik Hamann, Distinguished Researcher, and Chief Scientist for Geoinformatics at IBM.

Forecasts of the base variables - wind speed and global horizontal irradiance, as well as the resulting power output - allow for a view of a variety of time horizons, from minutes and hours ahead (for grid stability and dispatching resources) to a day ahead (optimizing plant availability), to several days ahead (scheduling maintenance).

With the availability of larger data sets, predictions can now go far beyond the weather to train algorithms to predict more remarkable outcomes. For example, how much extra power is consumed during a festive holiday, a large-scale international event, or how much altitude affects a community's energy consumption.

More accurate forecasting of variable renewable energy at shorter timescales enables generators and energy traders to better forecast output and bid in wholesale and balancing markets – and, importantly, to do so while avoiding penalties.

The earlier and more accurately you can predict, the more efficient it is for energy traders to rebalance their position. "I see AI as a way to deal with a lot more sites while using more granular and diverse data than traditional forecast methods," says Alex Howard,

Head of Strategy at Origami. "Ultimately, this means a higher financial return.

More accurate forecasting of variable renewable energy at shorter timescales enables generators and energy traders to better forecast output and bid in wholesale and balancing markets – and, importantly, to do so while avoiding penalties.

Meanwhile, AI algorithms with vast amounts of weather data can ensure optimal use of power grids by adapting operations to weather conditions at any time for grid operators. More accurate short-term forecasting can lead to better unit commitment and increased dispatch efficiency, improving reliability and lowering the need for operating reserves.

With AI, we can predict more accurately what renewables will do, allowing us to control other power plants more accurately, such as coal plants that take many hours to ramp up," says James Kelloway, Energy Intelligence Manager at National Grid ESO.

Cost savings can then be passed on. "What we want to avoid is turning off renewables," he adds. Renewables are not only greener, but they are usually cheaper in terms of price and system configuration.

Grid operators can optimize consumer energy consumption through a grid-stability lens, with AI ensuring that the power grid operates at optimal load. However, AI can be used by more than just transmission system operators; its application extends beyond central planning and can play a larger role on the grid's edge through machine-to-machine communication.

Electricity generated within a neighborhood grid or solar PV system can be used to improve reliability and combat grid congestion, which is associated with complex, decentralized systems with bi-directional electricity flow.

The earlier and more accurately you can forecast, the easier it is for energy traders to rebalance their positions. Ultimately, this means a higher financial return.

Accurate demand forecasting is also critical, and AI can help with this by optimizing economic load dispatch and improving demand-side management. With the increased installation of smart meters, demand data can now be sent to utility providers. AI algorithms can process data that is sent as frequently as hourly and accurately predict network load and consumption habits.

Utility bills can be reduced for consumers by AI systems predicting a building's thermal energy demand and producing heating and cooling at the appropriate times via home solar and battery systems optimization. Efficiency gains are combined with load shifting to times when electricity is cheapest, and the system includes renewable energy.

We can now predict when demand spikes will occur and discharge energy to keep customers' grid-supplied electricity below a certain set point, and thus help customers control energy costs without interrupting operations or requiring any involvement on their part," says Josh Lehman, Senior Director of Product Management at Stem in the United States. He goes on to say that the company's AI-powered software has increased customer savings by about 5% year on year.

The ability to understand consumers' habits and actions creates greater flexibility in a smart grid because AI algorithms can make predictions about a building's energy use 24 hours in advance, based on past experiences.

Battery storage also plays an important role in providing demand flexibility, with AI once again playing a key role.

Because storage batteries can be activated quickly and used to manage excessive peaks – as well as reduce the amount of backup energy required from diesel generators, coal-fired power plants, or other gas-fired "peaker" plants that are used at peak demand – AI can predict and make energy storage management decisions by taking into account forecast demand, renewable energy generation, prices, and network congestion, among other variables.

Battery owners can deploy their storage pack based on the compensation for the battery's services. Stem has created AI algorithms to map out energy usage and allow customers to track fluctuations in energy rates to make better use of storage.

The ability to understand consumers' habits and actions creates greater flexibility in a smart grid because AI algorithms can make predictions about a building's energy use 24 hours in advance, based on past experiences.

Similarly, AI is used in versatile battery storage systems by AMS, a US-based software-as-a-service platform provider, to optimize opportunities to purchase electricity from the grid when prices are low and then sell back to the market when prices are high. Another example is Australia's Hornsdale battery, which has 150MW and uses a Tesla-developed auto bidder AI algorithm, which has allowed the project to capture revenue streams five times higher than an energy trader, according to AMS.

AI can also help electricity providers with asset management operations and maintenance. AI algorithms can automatically detect mechanical failure disturbances in real-time, improving power system reliability and efficiency. Algorithms can learn to distinguish and precisely categorize normal operating data from defined system malfunctions by using sensor data.

"Unexpected disruptions across the industry can cost 3%-8% of capacity and $10 billion in annual lost production," says Brian Case, Chief Digital Officer at GE Renewable Energy. Its Predix software contains AI-based algorithms that can interpret industrial data to predict machine health and recommend actions to improve efficiency for assets like wind farms.

The ability of AI to detect system flaws immediately can also prevent a chain reaction. For example, if one power plant fails, the load on other power plants will experience an abrupt increase. As a result, the generators slow down and the frequency falls.

If the frequency falls below a certain level, the operator may be forced to cut off sections of the grid to keep the system stable. Because AI algorithms can make split-second decisions, appropriate, fully automated countermeasures can be implemented.

Unexpected disruptions in the industry can cost 3%-8% of capacity and US$10 billion in lost production each year.

The challenges of applying AI across the sector

Poor data, consumer mistrust, and regulatory obstacles could all be issues for the technology.

The potential for AI to be a game changer in the renewable energy sector is undeniable, but this does not mean that its wider application will be without challenges.

In today's digital age, some concerns relying too heavily on AI may leave energy networks vulnerable to cyber-attacks. In 2015, hackers knocked down 30 substations in Ukraine, leaving 230,000 people in the dark for six hours. A year later, a much smaller attack on a transmission station in Kyiv occurKyiv It is believed that the 2015 attack took months of planning and a team of dozens working in coordination and that it was largely the result of employees falling for a phishing campaign.

Another type of cyber-attack on power grids that have recently been deployed involves the use of vulnerabilities in firewall firmware. The North American Electric Reliability Corporation revealed in 2019 that the first attack on a US grid network occurred when an unnamed utility experienced a communication outage between its control center and generation sites. The outage was caused by an outside party rebooting the company's firewalls. Each communication failure lasted less than five minutes, but the attack lasted approximately ten hours.

However, the chances of another successful large-scale attack appear to be slim. Because there are no network connections between operational technology (OT) and information technology (IT) systems, they are much more difficult to infiltrate. Furthermore, because OT systems are more customized and esoteric, would-be hackers are less familiar with them.

If hackers were to gain access to operational networks, they would need to learn the equipment and configurations. Furthermore, regardless of the equipment setup, a utility has, manipulating its physical processes can necessitate real expertise, as well as months of additional effort and resources. Experts believe that the vast majority of grid-penetration incidents will be nothing more than spear phishing.

Data bias, audit, and ongoing verification of algorithms are performance issues that AI systems must consider when developing algorithms. Machine learning is extremely sensitive to bad data, and the adage "garbage in, garbage out" applies here. It is critical to take data and make it machine-readable so that quality is in, and quality out. Frequent data verification is required for trusted AI to ensure that algorithms remain valid over time and that machines do not deviate from the original algorithms as they learn.

Some concerns relying too heavily on AI may leave energy networks vulnerable to cyber-attacks. However, operational technology systems are isolated from IT systems, with no network connections between the two, making infiltration much more difficult.

That is not always as simple as it sounds. "AI may have some limitations in areas where there is no historical data to find the intelligence because it has never occurred or existed before," warns IBM's Hamann. "However, you can overcome these challenges by utilizing various, more and more selective data sources, as well as various techniques."

From a technological standpoint, reliance on cellular technologies would limit AI's potential in many emerging markets, particularly low-income ones, in rural and other underserved areas. Smart meters rely on constant data communication, so a lack of dependable connectivity is a significant impediment in areas with sparse or limited cellular network coverage.

As with any new technology, consumers are likely to be skeptical at first. Building owners and occupants are likely to be skeptical that the technology can reduce energy consumption or costs while maintaining energy services and comfort. To persuade customers to trust the technology, robust education and marketing programs will be required.

There are also regulatory barriers, such as the requirement that energy market rules allow for the trading of flexible demand on a large enough scale to allow commercial buildings to participate in the market. For example, in some energy markets, the minimum allowable bids are higher than the size of flexible loads likely to be offered by commercial buildings. Furthermore, some energy markets require participation fees, which may be a barrier to entry for small-scale participants.

Determining project viability with AI

How one company's use of image recognition is providing investors and developers with critical verified data.

The million-dollar question for investors and developers is whether a potential project will be financially viable. That question is now easier and faster to answer than ever before thanks to AI.

The opacity surrounding energy data has long hampered investors and developers. There is no shortage of publicly available open-access data on grids and power-generation assets, but developers require validated data to identify technical and financial risks for a prospective project to be profitable.

This is where image recognition, a primitive form of AI, can be extremely useful in validating open-access data. ENIAN, a UK software company, claims to have one of the world's largest renewable energy project databases, having collected publicly available data on power plants and grid assets, as well as their coordinates. The company runs a matching script across the data sets, and the AI is trained to recognize the appearance of a wind turbine. The AI examines millions of sets of wind turbine coordinates to determine which images and coordinates correspond.

AI can then be used to predict costs, with an enterprise platform easing project managers' workload. The platform provides datasets detailing assets' grid connections, distance to the nearest substation, existing power-generation assets in the area, and asset performance indicators based on reliable data retrieved from image recognition.

The opacity surrounding energy data has long hampered investors and developers. There is no shortage of open-access data on grids and power-generation assets in the public domain, but developers must identify technical and financial risks for a prospective project to be profitable.

AI augments projects, allowing managers to examine qualitative details such as how many competitors are in the area and whether or not other projects in the area have failed - and, if so, why. The data also reveals potential sites' solar irradiance and wind speeds, as well as an optimal route-selection estimate for connecting a power-generating asset to the grid, allowing project managers to create quick and accurate models of what a solar or wind farm can produce. The algorithm then generates a preliminary cash-flow model that indicates whether the project should be pursued further.

"Because there is so much uncertainty about where the nearest points of interconnection are, a project's available capacity, and who the owner is, having this data without relying on third parties is very useful."

For developers, operational excellence is the name of the game, and AI can help firms get a leg up on the competition by identifying profitable prospective projects faster. The ability to rapidly scale data collection and analysis via automation also frees up time for project managers to focus on closing deals faster, starting projects earlier, and moving timelines forward.

By providing verified data to project managers, projects become more predictable, efficient, and cost-effective, resulting in higher returns on investment.

While AI has been chastised for its impact on the labor market, the emphasis should be shifted to its ability to free skilled labor from monotonous tasks. "AI is coming for the tasks you despise, such as spending a lot of time processing data and validating data," says Bruner. The machine can step in and perform those routine tasks, enhancing everyone's capabilities."

Increasing research and development to improve the capabilities of artificial intelligence

Further research and development could find solutions to AI's limitations and reduce costs, as it did with solar.

AI and its accompanying emerging technologies, such as IoT, sensors, big data, and distributed ledger technology, are game changers in the renewable energy sector. Prediction capability through demand forecasting and asset management, combined with increased automation providing operational excellence, are already resulting in significant cost savings, higher yields, and higher returns on investment.

R&D in the solar industry has driven down prices, and further R&D in AI has the potential to drastically lower costs while its capabilities grow and solutions to its limitations emerge. Governments are recognizing this as well, with the US Department of Energy announcing US$37 million in AI R&D funding in August 2020. The UK is also funding several new research hubs to develop robotic technology to improve offshore wind safety.

"We are now at the point where the most sophisticated market participants are transforming proofs of concept into reality, scalable applications of the technology," Howard of Origami says, adding that he expects these applications to de-risk the area for others.

The most sophisticated market participants are now transforming proofs of concept into reality, scalable applications of the technology.

The future of work

How AI will change the job market

We previously discovered that approximately half of the activities that people are paid to do around the world could theoretically be automated using currently demonstrated technologies. Few occupations—less than 5%—consist of activities that can be completely automated.

However, at least one-third of the constituent activities in approximately 60% of occupations could be automated, implying significant workplace transformations and changes for all workers.

While technical feasibility is important, it is not the only factor influencing the pace and extent of automation adoption. Other considerations include the cost of developing and deploying automation solutions for specific workplace applications, labor-market dynamics (including labor quality and quantity and associated wages), the benefits of automation beyond labor substitution, and regulatory and social acceptance.

Taking these factors into account, our new research estimates that between 0% and 30% of global labor hours could be automated by 2030, depending on the rate of adoption.

We primarily employ the middle point of our scenario range, which is the automation of 15% of current activities. The results vary greatly by country, reflecting the mix of activities currently performed by workers as well as the prevailing wage rates.

The potential impact of automation on employment varies according to occupation and industry (see interactive above). Physical activities in predictable environments, such as operating machinery and preparing fast food, are particularly vulnerable to automation. Data collection and processing are two other categories of activities that machines are increasingly capable of doing better and faster. This has the potential to displace a significant amount of labor, such as in mortgage origination, paralegal work, accounting, and back-office transaction processing.

However, it is important to note that even if some tasks are automated, employment in those occupations may not decline; rather, workers may perform new tasks.

Automation will have a smaller impact on jobs that require managing people, applying expertise, and social interactions, where machines are currently incapable of matching human performance.

Jobs in unpredictable environments, such as gardeners, plumbers, or child- and eldercare providers, will also see less automation by 2030, because they are technically difficult to automate and often command lower wages, making automation a less appealing business proposition.

What are possible scenarios for employment growth?

Workers who are displaced by automation are easily identified, whereas new jobs created indirectly by technology are less visible and spread across different industries and geographies. We simulate some potential sources of new labor demand that could drive job creation through 2030, even after accounting for automation.

Stay current on your favorite topics

We only model a trendline scenario for the first three trends based on current spending and investment trends observed across countries.

Rising incomes and consumption, particularly in emerging markets

We previously estimated that global consumption could increase by $23 trillion between 2015 and 2030, with the majority of this coming from emerging-market consumers. These new consumers' effects will be felt not only in the countries where the income is generated but also in the economies that export to these countries. Globally, we estimate that rising incomes alone could generate 250 million to 280 million new jobs, with an additional 50 million to 85 million jobs generated by increased health and education spending.

Aging populations

There will be at least 300 million more people aged 65 and older by 2030 than there were in 2014. As people get older, their spending habits change, with a noticeable increase in spending on healthcare and other personal services. In many countries, this will result in significant new demand for a variety of occupations, including doctors, nurses, and health technicians, as well as home-health aides, personal-care aides, and nursing assistants. Globally, we estimate that healthcare and aging-related jobs will increase by 50 million to 85 million by 2030.

Development and deployment of technology

Jobs in the development and deployment of new technologies may also expand. Between 2015 and 2030, total technology spending could increase by more than 50%. Approximately half would be spent on information-technology services. The number of people employed in these occupations is small in comparison to those in healthcare or construction, but they pay well. We estimate that by 2030, this trend will have created 20 million to 50 million jobs worldwide.

We model both a trendline scenario and a step-up scenario for the next three trends, assuming additional investments in some areas based on explicit choices by governments, business leaders, and individuals to create more jobs.

Investments in infrastructure and buildings

Infrastructure and buildings are two areas of historic underspending that, if action is taken to bridge infrastructure gaps and address housing shortages, could generate significant additional labor demand. In the trendline scenario, up to 80 million new jobs could be created, and in the step-up scenario, up to 200 million, more could be created if the investment is accelerated. Architects, engineers, electricians, carpenters, and other skilled tradespeople, as well as construction workers, hold these positions.

Renewable energy, energy efficiency, and climate adaptation investments

Renewable energy investments, such as wind and solar; energy-efficiency technologies; and climate change adaptation and mitigation may create new demand for workers in a variety of occupations, including manufacturing, construction, and installation. In the trendline scenario, these investments could generate up to ten million new jobs, while the step-up scenario could generate up to ten million additional jobs globally.

The marketization of previously unpaid domestic work

The final trend we will look at is the ability to pay for services that replace currently unpaid and primarily domestic work. This so-called "marketization" of previously unpaid work is already common in advanced economies, and rising female labor-force participation around the world may accelerate the trend. We estimate that this could generate 50 million to 90 million jobs worldwide, primarily in childcare, early childhood education, cleaning, cooking, and gardening.

When we look at the net changes in job growth across all countries, the following categories have the highest percentage of job growth net of automation:

1. Healthcare providers
2. Engineers, scientists, accountants, and analysts are examples of professionals.
3. IT specialists and other technology experts
4. Managers and executives whose jobs cannot be easily automated
5. Educators, particularly in developing countries with young populations
6. "Creatives," a small but growing category of artists, performers, and entertainers who will be in demand as incomes rise and demand for leisure and recreation increases.
7. Builders and related professions, particularly in the case of increased infrastructure and building investment
8. Home-health aides and gardeners are examples of manual and service jobs in unpredictable environments.

Upcoming workforce transitions could be very large

Changes in net occupational growth or decline imply that a large number of people may need to change occupations and learn new skills in the coming years. The shift could be on a scale not seen since the early 1900s labor force transition out of agriculture in the United States, Europe, and, more recently, China.

Between 75 and 375 million people may need to change occupations and learn new skills.

Based on our midpoint and earliest (that is, the most rapid) automation adoption scenarios, we estimate that between 400 million and 800 million people worldwide may be displaced by automation and will need to find new jobs by 2030. Based on our scenarios of future labor demand and the net impact of automation, as described in the following section, new jobs will become available.

Will there be enough work in the future?

Given the possibility of automation, there is growing concerned about whether there will be enough jobs for workers. History suggests that such fears are unfounded: labor markets adjust to changes in demand for workers caused by technological disruptions over time, albeit with depressed real wages at times.

We address the question of the future of work through two sets of analyses: one based on modeling a limited number of previously described catalysts of new labor demand and automation, and the other based on a macroeconomic model of the economy that incorporates dynamic interactions among variables.

If history is any guide, we can also expect that 8 to 9 percent of 2030 labor demand will be in previously unknown occupations.

Both analyses lead us to the conclusion that, with sufficient economic growth, innovation, and investment, there can be enough new job creation to offset the impact of automation, though additional investments will be required in some advanced economies, according to our step-up scenario, to reduce the risk of job shortages.

A larger challenge will be ensuring that employees have the necessary skills and support to transition to new jobs. Countries that fail to manage this transition risk seeing rising unemployment and wage stagnation.

The magnitude of future job creation as a result of the previously described trends, as well as the impact of automation on the workforce, varies greatly by country, depending on four factors.

Wage level

Higher wages strengthen the business case for automation adoption. However, low-wage countries may be affected as well if companies use automation to improve quality, tighten production control, move production closer to end consumers in high-wage countries, or for other reasons other than cost reduction.

Demand growth

Economic growth is necessary for job creation; stagnant or slowly growing economies create few, if any, net new jobs. Countries with stronger economic and productivity growth, as well as greater innovation, are expected to experience more new labor demand.

Demographics

If young people are employed, countries with a rapidly growing workforce, such as India, may benefit from a "demographic dividend" that boosts GDP growth. Countries with a shrinking workforce, such as Japan, can expect lower GDP growth in the future if only productivity grows.

A mix of economic sectors and occupations

Countries' automation potential reflects the mix of economic sectors and jobs within each sector. Japan, for example, has a higher automation potential than the US because the weight of highly automatable sectors, such as manufacturing, is greater.

Automation will affect countries in different ways

The four factors mentioned above combined to produce different forecasts for the future of work in each country (see interactive heat map). Japan is wealthy, but its economy is expected to grow slowly through 2030. It is confronted with a combination of slower job creation due to economic expansion and a large share of work that can be automated due to high wages and the structure of its economy.

However, Japan's workforce will shrink by four million people by 2030. In the step-up scenario, and taking into account the jobs in new occupations that we cannot imagine today, Japan's net job change could be roughly balanced.

Although the United States and Germany may face significant workforce displacement from automation by 2030, their projected future growth—and thus new job creation—is higher. The United States has a growing workforce, and it is roughly balanced in the step-up scenario, with innovations leading to new types of occupations and work. Even in the trendline scenario, Germany's workforce will decline by three million people by 2030, but there will be more than enough labor demand to employ all of its workers.

India, on the other hand, is a rapidly growing developing country with relatively modest potential for automation over the next 15 years due to low wage rates. According to our analysis, most occupational categories in India are expected to grow, reflecting the country's potential for rapid economic growth.

However, India's labor force is expected to grow by 138 million people, or roughly 30%, by 2030. By investing in our step-up scenario, India could create enough new jobs to offset automation and employ these new entrants.

Because China and Mexico have higher wages than India, they are more likely to see increased automation. China is still expected to have robust economic growth and a shrinking workforce; China's problem, like Germany's, could be a labor shortage.

Mexico's projected rate of future economic expansion is lower, and it could benefit from job creation in the step-up scenario, as well as innovation in new occupations and activities, to fully utilize its workforce.

To avoid rising unemployment, displaced workers must be quickly reemployed.

We use a general equilibrium model that takes into account the economic impacts of automation as well as dynamic interactions to model the impact of automation on overall employment and wages. At least three distinct economic effects result from automation. The potential displacement of labor has received the most attention. However, automation may increase labor productivity: firms use automation only when it allows them to produce more or higher-quality output with the same or fewer inputs (including material, energy, and labor inputs).

The third effect is that automation adoption increases economic investment, which boosts short-term GDP growth. We simulate all three effects. Based on historical data, we also generate different scenarios for how quickly displaced workers find new jobs.

The findings show that, in almost all scenarios, the six countries covered by our report (China, Germany, India, Japan, Mexico, and the United States) can expect to be at or near full employment by 2030. However, the model also emphasizes the importance of quickly re-employing displaced workers.

If displaced workers can be reemployed within a year, our model predicts that automation will boost the overall economy: full employment will be maintained in both the short and long term, wages will grow faster than in the baseline model, and productivity will be higher.

However, when some displaced workers take years to find new employment, unemployment rises in the short to medium term. The labor market adjusts over time, and unemployment falls, but average wage growth is slower. Average wages in these scenarios are lower in 2030 than in the baseline model, which could dampen aggregate demand and long-term growth.

What will automation mean for skills and wages?

In general, the current educational requirements for potential growth occupations are higher than those for jobs displaced by automation. Automation is causing a net decline in occupations that currently require only a secondary education or less in advanced economies, while occupations requiring college degrees or higher are growing.

We find higher labor demand for all education levels in India and other emerging economies, with the newest jobs in occupations requiring a secondary education, but the fastest rate of job growth will be in occupations currently requiring a college or advanced degree.

Workers of the future will devote more time to tasks that machines are less capable of performing, such as managing people, applying expertise, and communicating with others. They will devote less time to predictable physical activities and data collection and processing, where machines already outperform humans. The required skills and capabilities will also shift, necessitating more social and emotional skills as well as advanced cognitive abilities such as logical reasoning and creativity.

Wages in declining occupations may stagnate or fall. Although we do not model changes in relative wages across occupations, the basic economics of labor supply and demand suggests that this should be the case for occupations with declining labor demand.

According to our analysis, the majority of job growth in the United States and other advanced economies will be in occupations currently at the top of the wage distribution. Some low-wage occupations, such as nursing assistants and teaching assistants, will see increases, while a wide range of middle-income occupations will see significant job losses.

Income polarization may persist. Increased investments in infrastructure, buildings, and energy transitions, for example, could help create additional demand for middle-wage jobs like construction workers in advanced economies.

In emerging economies such as China and India, where our scenarios show that middle-wage jobs such as retail salespeople and teachers will grow the most as these economies develop, the wage-trend picture is quite different. This implies that their consumer class will continue to expand in the coming decades.

How will we handle the impending workforce transitions?

The benefits of AI and automation to users and businesses, as well as the economic growth that could result from their productivity contributions, are compelling. They will not only contribute to dynamic economies that create jobs but will also aid in the creation of economic surpluses that will allow societies to address the unavoidable workforce transitions.

When confronted with the magnitude of worker transitions described here, one reaction might be to try to slow the pace and scope of adoption to maintain the status quo. However, this would be a mistake. Slower adoption may limit the scale of workforce transitions, but it will reduce the contributions of these technologies to business dynamism and economic growth. We must embrace these technologies while also addressing the workforce transitions and challenges that they bring. Many countries may need a Marshall Plan-scale initiative, involving sustained investment, new training models, programs to ease worker transitions, income support, and collaboration between the public and private sectors.

All societies will need to address four critical issues.

Maintaining strong economic growth to fuel job creation

Maintaining robust aggregate demand growth, as well as encouraging the new business formation and innovation, is critical to supporting job creation.

Fiscal and monetary policies that ensure adequate aggregate demand, as well as the encouragement of business investment and innovation, will be critical. Targeted initiatives in specific sectors, such as increased investments in infrastructure and energy transitions, could also be beneficial.

Job retraining and workforce skill development are being scaled and reimagined.

Job retraining and enabling individuals to learn marketable new skills throughout their lives will be a critical challenge—and, in some countries, the primary challenge. Mid-career retraining will become increasingly important as the skill set required for a successful career change evolves. Businesses can lead in some areas, such as on-the-job training and providing opportunities for employees to advance their skills.

Increasing the dynamism of the business and labor markets, including mobility

Greater labor market fluidity will be required to manage the difficult transitions that we anticipate. This includes restoring advanced economies' now-dwindling labor mobility. Digital talent platforms can promote fluidity by connecting workers with companies looking for their skills and providing a plethora of new job opportunities for those willing to take them. Policymakers in countries with rigid labor markets can learn from countries that have deregulated their labor markets, such as Germany, which transformed its federal unemployment agency into a powerful job-matching entity.

Policymakers Workers receive some transitional assistance.

Income support and other forms of transition assistance will be critical in assisting displaced workers to find gainful employment. Aside from retraining, a variety of policies, such as unemployment insurance, public assistance in finding work, and portable benefits that follow workers between jobs, can be beneficial.

Wages for many occupations can be depressed for a while during workforce transitions, as history has shown. To support aggregate demand and ensure societal fairness, more permanent policies to supplement work incomes may be required. More comprehensive minimum-wage policies, universal basic income, and wage increases tied to productivity growth are all potential solutions under consideration.

Policymakers, business leaders, and individual workers all have important and constructive roles to play in smoothing out future workforce transitions. History demonstrates that when confronted with monumental challenges, societies around the world frequently rise to the occasion to ensure the well-being of their citizens.

However, investments and policies to support the workforce have dwindled over the last few decades. Most Organization for Economic Cooperation and Development member countries have reduced public spending on labor-force training and support (OECD). In the last century, educational models have remained largely unchanged. It is now critical for governments to prioritize workforce transitions and job creation to reverse these trends.

In a world where the role and meaning of work begin to shift, we will all require creative visions for how our lives are organized and valued in the future.

Businesses will be on the front lines of workplace transformation. This will necessitate them retooling their business processes as well as reevaluating their talent strategies and workforce needs, carefully considering which individuals are required, which can be redeployed to other jobs, and where new talent may be needed. Many businesses are discovering that it is both in their self-interest and part of their social responsibility to train and prepare workers for a new world of work.

Individuals must also be prepared for a rapidly changing work environment. Acquiring new in-demand skills and resetting intuition about the working world will be critical for their well-being. Human labor will be in demand, but workers everywhere will need to reconsider traditional notions of where they work, how they work, and what talents and capabilities they bring to that work.

Can AI predict and prevent natural disasters?

Every country's top priority should be AI Disaster Response and Risk Management, as disasters can take many different forms. We must be prepared for natural disasters such as hurricanes and wildfires, as well as pandemics and terrorist attacks. A disaster can have devastating consequences for both the people affected and the economy. Artificial intelligence (AI), particularly machine learning (ML), plays an important role in disaster risk reduction (DRR), from forecasting extreme events to developing risk mitigation strategies and providing real-time situational awareness and decision support.

It is critical to have a disaster risk management strategy in place to minimize the damage caused by disasters. Many experts believe artificial intelligence (AI) can help with disaster response and risk management.

Artificial Intelligence / Machine Learning for Disaster Response and Recovery

First, consider how AI and machine learning (ML) can assist when disaster strikes. Algorithms are used in artificial intelligence to learn from data. Machine learning is a type of artificial intelligence that enables computer systems to learn from experience without being programmed to do so.

First responders in the context of disaster response can use AI and ML for a variety of tasks, including:

Automated damage assessment

Damage assessment is one of the first steps in any disaster response. This entails dispatching assessor teams to assess the extent of the damage. Damage assessment using AI and ML can help to accelerate this process.

To identify damaged buildings, for example, we can use computer vision algorithms to analyze images and videos. This data can then be used to create maps of the affected areas. Furthermore, businesses can use AI to process large amounts of data from various sources (e.g., social media, and satellite images). This provides a complete picture of the disaster's damage.

Google has one such AI that uses data from the most recent earthquakes, such as:

- Haiti (2010)
- Mexico City (2017)
- Indonesia (2018)

Responders can better understand the gravity of the disaster situation by using AI for damage assessment.

Predictive analytics for evacuation

Another way AI can assist during a disaster is to use predictive analytics to predict when and where an evacuation may be required. As an example, consider an erupting volcano.

Predictive analytics can be used to analyze data from seismic sensors, weather data, and satellite images.

This data can then be used by experts to build a model that predicts how an eruption will unfold. Knowing if it will be violent enough to necessitate an evacuation and when it might occur allows authorities to efficiently prepare for the disaster.

Furthermore, predictive analytics can be used to analyze social media data. This information can be used to track rumors about an impending disaster. Responders can get a head start on evacuations and other response measures by using AI-based methods to monitor social media.

Routing of emergency resources

Time is of the essence during a disaster. Many of the tasks that must be completed during a disaster response can be accelerated. This has the potential to save lives and reduce damage. Transfer learning can be used to develop models capable of analyzing satellite images and identifying areas of damage. This information can then be used by relevant authorities to deploy emergency services.

Intelligent search algorithms are used to determine the best evacuation route. We can ensure that emergency resources are deployed more efficiently and effectively by using AI to route them. Furthermore, we can use AI-powered solutions to forecast the path of a natural disaster.

A Geographic Information System (GIS) can also be used to help with routing. QGIS, for example, can be used to create maps that show the locations of evacuation centers and first responders.

Prevention

Disaster risk management entails more than just response and recovery. It is also a matter of prevention. Artificial intelligence can detect risk factors that could result in a disaster. It can, for example, use machine learning to analyze historical data to identify patterns that may indicate an impending disaster.

The methods used to collect this data have become more sophisticated. Drones and sensors, for example, can help to collect data more efficiently. This data can then be processed by AI to provide insights that can aid in the prevention of severe damage from natural disasters.

In that case, cities can implement disaster preparedness programs such as early warning systems to lessen the impact of the disaster.

Real-Time Data and the Internet of Things

Another way AI can aid in disaster response is through the provision of real-time data. In a nutshell, the Internet of Things (IoT) is a network of physical devices, vehicles, and household appliances that are linked to the internet. These devices have sensors that collect information about their surroundings. This data is then processed and analyzed in real-time by AI to provide insights.

First responders are frequently forced to rely on information that is hours or even days old. This can make making informed decisions about where to deploy resources difficult.

The Internet of Things has the potential to collect real-time data that can be used to improve disaster response. Government leaders, for example, can place sensors in high-risk areas to monitor conditions and provide early warning of impending danger.

There are also flood monitoring system networks that share real-time data to help predict and prepare for floods. It is critical to have up-to-date information about the disaster to respond effectively.

Engaging the Whole Community

Engaging the entire community is the best way to improve disaster response. Government agencies, businesses, non-profits, and individuals are all included. Each of these organizations has something to offer the disaster response effort. AI-powered methods can more easily involve the entire community in disaster response efforts.

Businesses, for example, can use AI to monitor social media for early warnings of impending disasters. AI can be used by emergency management systems to identify people in need of assistance and deploy resources from city infrastructure accordingly.

During a disaster, city departments can use artificial intelligence to predict traffic patterns and plan the best evacuation route. Due to gridlock, people were stranded for days in disasters such as Hurricane Sandy.

We can avoid future gridlock by using artificial intelligence to predict traffic patterns.

If evacuation is not an option, AI can be used to identify safe areas for shelter.

Staying a Step Ahead of Disasters

Artificial intelligence-based disaster response and risk management methods can assist us in staying one step ahead of disasters. We can evacuate people and deploy resources ahead of time by using AI to predict the path of a disaster.

We can use deep learning techniques and reinforcement learning to predict the most likely path of a hurricane if we know it will hit a specific area. In this case, behavior learning works best because it can learn from past data to predict future behavior.

Biases in training data can distort results depending on the collection methods used. Because machine learning is primarily used to analyze large data sets, training biases are sometimes overlooked. In the case of rare disasters such as hurricanes, the training data set is usually insufficient to accurately predict the storm's path.

Finally, AI can improve humanitarian mapping efforts by using machine learning to automatically map the affected area. This is especially useful in large-scale disasters like earthquakes, where a large amount of data must be processed quickly. These humanitarian mapping efforts can help first responders plan the best way to deploy resources.

Public/Private Partnerships Are Vital for Adequate Disaster Response

It is also important to note that public-private partnerships are essential for effective disaster response. The government cannot do everything, and private businesses frequently have the resources and expertise to fill in the gaps.

Many technology companies have started to provide training materials and services to assist government agencies in improving their disaster response efforts. When private companies participate in disaster response, there are ethical considerations to be considered, but these partnerships can be a force for good in the long run.

AI emergency management systems are being developed in a variety of ways. We want to understand the effects of these tragedies on city departments before a disaster occurs. Behavior learning is an excellent example of how AI can be applied in this manner.

We can use AI to create city infrastructure models and simulate various disasters to see how the city would react. These simulations can assist us in identifying flaws in city infrastructure and making changes before a disaster strikes.

Finally, public-private partnerships like these can help build a more resilient community in the face of future disasters. We can ensure that the necessary resources are available to respond effectively to any disaster by working together.

Conclusion

Disaster risk management is a multifaceted and complex issue. AI and machine learning can aid in disaster response in a variety of ways. AI can make a significant difference in disaster mitigation, from automated damage assessment to predictive analytics for evacuation

AI-powered VA are changing the way we interact with

A virtual assistant is an artificial intelligence-powered application program that accepts voice commands and executes them. The VA tools can perform a variety of tasks, such as scheduling appointments, sending emails and messages, opening applications, playing music, and setting alarm clocks. The core processing for these applications is provided by integrating AI technologies such as machine learning and natural language processing, and these tools are now more accurate than ever.

Aside from that, virtual assistant software is used to power IoT devices and perform complex tasks such as checking the status of home devices, closing and opening doors, turning on lights and air conditioning, checking the news, finding restaurants, and so on. VA technology advancements have created new opportunities for advanced solutions across domains.

The benefits of AI virtual assistant software

Companies and end-users benefit greatly from feature-rich, AI-based virtual assistant software applications. As a business owner, you want to provide your potential customers with the best service possible. By incorporating VA software into your company's workflow, you can provide better service to your customers while also benefiting from a more accurate data analytics module.

Let's look at some of the benefits you get from the VA tool.

Customer service is available 24 hours a day, seven days a week.

The virtual assistant tool provides customer support 24 hours a day, seven days a week without the need for human intervention. The chatbot is an excellent example of a VA tool, and advanced chatbots can provide high-quality assistance with various products and services. They also collect and record pertinent information from customers. A chatbot tool reduces costs and human effort while improving customer service through faster response times.

Ease of access

Customers' ease of access and convenience is one of the most significant benefits of deploying virtual assistant tools. As a result, today's major corporations, including Google, Apple, Tesla, Samsung, and Amazon, are constantly working to improve their virtual assistant tools. A sophisticated VA tool provides efficient solutions in various customer access modules and is likely to play a more advanced role in future business workflow

Higher engagement

The virtual assistant applications also improve customer engagement through a wide range of highly evolved services and ease of access. One of any company's or business's goals is to provide high levels of customer satisfaction through its products and services.

The use of VA tools aids in the delivery of advanced solutions with greater accuracy, which leads to improved customer engagement. Higher engagement is directly proportional to higher conversion rates and sales. As a result, if you want to improve your customer service, you should think about incorporating a dependable virtual assistant into your framework.

Reduced costs

The virtual assistant tool assists businesses and companies in lowering their expenditure on various tasks by automating them with advanced AI solutions in the form of virtual assistants. These VA tools provide a more efficient way of handling administrative tasks and significantly reduce human effort, resulting in significant cost savings. Effective VA tools and software systems are the future of industry workflow, providing numerous benefits, one of which is lower costs.

Monetization opportunities

You can create a highly functional and scalable virtual assistant tool for use across multiple devices and ecosystems. Creating a virtual assistant tool for end-users can assist businesses in generating multiple monetization opportunities as different clients integrate these VA tools into their devices and workflows. Amazon Alexa, for example, generates significant revenue by allowing clients to integrate Alexa skills into their respective work frames.

Examples of AI virtual assistant tools

Numerous highly efficient and feature-rich virtual assistant tools are available on the market, offering a variety of functionality and benefits to end users. Here are some of the most notable ones, as well as how they have impacted the digital ecosystem.

Google Home

Google Home is a comprehensive virtual assistant tool that communicates with users via voice commands and has a wide range of capabilities. Users of Google Home can perform a variety of tasks, such as playing music, sending messages and emails, scheduling appointments, calling people, playing games, and so on. Google Home can also control smart home devices such as security systems, lights, thermostats, and cameras.

Amazon Alexa

Amazon Alexa is a prime example of VA technology that improves productivity and ease of access for end users. Alexa supports voice interaction and performs a variety of tasks based on user input. Users can use Alexa to listen to music, listen to podcasts, read news, and get weather updates, among other things. Alexa is platform and operating system agnostic, providing a high level of portability.

Siri

Siri is an Apple personal digital assistant tool that is primarily integrated with iOS and mac devices and is used to perform a variety of functions. Among other things, Siri can provide weather updates, check the news, play music, call users, book movie tickets, search for flights, get traffic updates, and set alarms.

Siri can also perform Google searches, get sports-related news, scores, and stats, perform mathematical calculations, facetime with friends, and take notes. With ever-changing data, AI virtual assistant tools like Siri are constantly improving and providing more advanced capabilities to end users.

Mitsuko

Mitsuko is a popular virtual assistant chatbot that can effectively converse with customers by utilizing natural language processing and machine learning algorithms. Many businesses are increasingly utilizing chatbot applications for customer service and providing users with 24/7 access. Chatbot applications have advanced dramatically in recent years, and chatbots are now far more accurate and efficient than ever before.

Mitsuko can be integrated with various platforms and trained to recognize speech patterns, allowing it to provide intelligent responses based on specific requirements. The potential for chatbot applications is enormous, and we can expect to see greater integration of chatbot tools into the daily workflow of various businesses and companies.

Developing an AI virtual assistant software system

As we've seen, several ways developing a highly scalable virtual assistant software system can benefit your company. Installation of compatible libraries and software modules for implementing the speech recognition system is required before the development process.

Hiring NLP and AI engineers with the necessary experience to manage your custom development requirements is the best way to build highly functional virtual assistant software. Depending on your objectives and needs, you can create various VA tools with varying scopes. This includes website navigation and search assistance, chatbot integration, administrative assistance, and more advanced virtual assistant versions.

Before developing the VA tool, you must identify the application's key functionalities, problems that the tool can solve, budgeting requirements, and how the overall investment can help you with increased productivity and higher leads or sales. After you've documented the requirements and analyzed the entire process, you can begin hiring relevant engineers or developers who share your vision and can build a refined product that is scalable in response to changing requirements.

Wrapping up

Virtual assistant software has grown in popularity in recent years and is expected to evolve into a more efficient and better module in the future. This AI-powered application has enormous potential to provide advanced solutions to users, making this space even more exciting. Having your VA tool is a no-brainer with a slew of benefits and potential future scalability.

Turing is the ideal place to build a high-quality team of dependable developers to lead your virtual assistant software development project. Our AI-powered Intelligent Talent Cloud system finds vets, matches, and manages the world's best remote developers. Join the 300+ companies that rely on Turing to hire Silicon Valley-caliber software developers all over the world.

The role of AI in cybersecurity

opportunities and challenges

Privacy is an illusion, while security is a requirement. By the time we reach the third decade of the twenty-first century, the world has been inundated with rapid scientific and technological progress. Nothing appears to be a mere fable or fiction any longer, and intelligence now measures diligence, which is less human and more machine oriented. However, because not everything is drizzled maple syrup over your bowl of overnight oats, the consequences in the form of security breaches and privacy violations are pancakes at a hefty price, on sale.

Cybersecurity is a concern, and the introduction of artificial intelligence appears to be assisting in this regard. Will it, however, be effective? We will learn about the role of artificial intelligence in cyber security in this article. Furthermore, let us track the predicted future of AI in cyber security.

Role of Artificial Intelligence in Cyber Security

AI systems operate autonomously and independently. Artificial intelligence solutions' future cannot be predicted; however, they should not be relied on entirely. The best way to think about it is as an intelligent and powerful soldier capable of making calculations and acting intuitively on the battlefield. Nonetheless, machine learning increases the effectiveness of the defensive force. As we progress through this article, we will learn about the role artificial intelligence plays in enabling cyber security, as well as the future of AI in cyber security. Before we get there, let's define cybersecurity.

Cyber Security

To protect against cyberattacks, cybersecurity is a practice that ensures the security of data stored on any electronic device that is connected to the internet.

It refers to the safeguarding and defense of computing systems against all types of digital threats and malicious attacks at the hardware, software, and data levels through the use of programs and processes.

Furthermore, the increasing use of IoT devices by consumers increases the potential risks to any person's or group's confidential and sensitive information. As a result, cybersecurity is a non-negotiable tool.

Cybersecurity has various components based on the type of security it provides, such as application security, network security, information or data security, cloud security, operational security, and so on.

Artificial Intelligence

Artificial intelligence refers to algorithms that are designed to mimic human intelligence to perform real-time tasks and improve by utilizing machine learning capabilities to adapt to new sets of information in the form of texts, audio, and video and process them on an integrated hardware and software foundation. AI programs consume massive amounts of data, analyze it for correlations and patterns, and generate their periodic inputs for a variety of situations.

AI is a repository of domain-specific knowledge that operates in three modes:

- Intelligence Assist
- Intelligence Augmented

- Intelligent Autonomous Systems

Artificial Intelligence in Cybersecurity

Cybersecurity, as an impromptu action, emphasizes the importance of constantly monitoring and addressing threats before they can cause any damage to the system. As a result, incorporating the role of artificial intelligence in cyber security not only automates manual force processes but also improves workflow accuracy and speed. This enables you to maintain security more efficiently.

Even though we have no doubts about human intelligence, AI does provide significant benefits to organizations that incorporate it into their defense programs. Given human limitations, it is impossible to identify new malware variants, phishing techniques, and every single threat faced by an organization and its cloud-based services. Furthermore, recognizing the potential of a threat is much more difficult due to the intensity and vulnerabilities it may attract to a server. In response to a threat, an unknown, undetected threat may cause massive damage to a system.

There are numerous advantages to AI Cyber Security that we can discuss. We will also discuss artificial intelligence and cybersecurity opportunities and challenges.

Data Asset Inventories

AI is a class of expert systems that use deep learning capabilities to access and accurately inventory all devices, users, and applications that run on them. This allows it to provide a data repository containing all of the information within an enterprise to better categorize and manage the data assets.

Securing Authentication

AI protects personal information on a device, such as usernames and passwords, credit card numbers, IDs, and so on. It is used by multiple commercial websites active across a business. They implement an additional layer of security to protect this information from infringements such as various types of malwares, viruses, worms, and trojans.

AI Identifies Unknown Threats

Sophistication with time includes not only security but also breaches. Every year, hundreds of millions of pests come to life. Finally, any obsolescence in the security system could expose the device to threats. By incorporating artificial intelligence into cyber security, it is possible to provide robust security by accurately assessing and responding to both existing and unknown threats. This AI-driven approach aids in the defense against the ever-changing landscape of cyber threats.

Monitors Traffic and Detects Anomalies

Even in a medium-sized organization, there is a lot of data exchange on a server, especially when there are multiple servers on the network between businesses and customers. Unauthorized access jeopardizes privacy and security. The data that travels across an organization's network may encounter potential risks that must be identified and prevented from causing any action. AI is the ideal solution for security professionals to independently evaluate traffic and ensure data security.

Intelligent Intelligence Over Time

Artificial Intelligence can improve over time by combining machine learning and deep learning capabilities. It is constantly evolving and updating itself based on ongoing information analysis. It analyzes patterns in an organization's network and clusters them according to its algorithm, allowing it to detect any future deviations or unrecognized patterns dynamically.

Endpoint Protection from Penetrations

The proliferation of devices within an organization makes maintaining security difficult. Antivirus software and Virtual Private Networks (VPNs) form a multi-layered defense shield to protect systems from potential threats at both the hardware and software levels.

Risk Protection

Because IT assets, both tangible and ethereal, are constantly targeted by cybercriminals, they require the assistance of AI systems. Furthermore, the intensity of hacking has increased to the point where any device can be remotely accessed and used from any distance if hacked. AI can predict and track upcoming cyberattacks and prepare suspect sites accordingly.

Bot Blocking

The role of artificial intelligence in cyber security also includes bot detection. Every organization in the sales and service sectors uses bots to conduct conversations. Bot comprehension poses risks to company systems and generates traffic. AI distinguishes between permissible and safe bots and eliminates malicious bots.

Better Risk Management

In today's world, speed is everything, and systems always appreciate quick evaluation and defense against infiltrations. To give our readers an idea, according to reports, the average number of threats received by an organization per day is around 200,000. The ability of an individual to recognize, understand, verify, and resolve a problem takes much longer than a previously generated algorithmic calculation. This reduces the force's workload while also assisting in the identification of weak points in a system that can be used to solve problems.

Better Overall Security

Malware, ransomware, hacking, and denial-of-service attacks are common threats to business organizations. AI prioritizes security measures against all of these threats and provides comprehensive protection. AI makes logical connections between risks and unauthorized IP addresses, resulting in real-time logical and data-driven insights. These help security professionals respond to attacks up to 60 times faster.

Retrieve Systems and Analyze the Root Cause

It can be refunded for the entire amount of its data if there is a system breach that results in data loss. Furthermore, the root cause of the attack can be identified and investigated with a deeper analysis.

Automated Security

Security automation occurs when Artificial Intelligence employs machine learning to automate similar security tasks such as patch management and incident response. As a result, the overburdening of human resources required to specify and supervise the task of security chambers can be reduced. AI could help to improve automation in standalone security systems. It would require organizations to defend against threats in real-time, even if manual operators were unavailable.

Artificial Intelligence Way to Future Cybersecurity

What more could an organization want from an intelligent agent that quickly solves side-lines and shoots away user abnormalities, examines hidden threats in millions of lines of code faster than expected, or detects malware attacks? The goal of artificial intelligence in cybersecurity is to detect malicious attacks and attempts as quickly as possible. We discovered the importance of artificial intelligence in cyber security. Finally, we can confidently state that the future of AI in cyber security is bright and clear.

The soaring technological revolution in the industrial sector is a gift basket offered to cybersecurity, transforming it from an action plan into a challenge to monitor threats around millions of globally connected devices. The shift in organizational behavior is directly related to the paradigm shift from old traditional structures to innovations in the form of smart devices, automated machinery, and advanced computing. The advancement of IoT, cloud computing, robots, and other technologies has highlighted the importance of incorporating AI into cybersecurity solutions.

IT industries are overburdened with resources to protect critical assets from a slew of attacks. AI and machine learning work together to process data and detect deviations in the behavior of the IoT ecosystem, keeping security alert and developing endpoint detection technologies.

AI cybersecurity solutions strive to provide the highest level of security protection required to counter threats, especially for government and national security agencies that have no room for error because any breach could have catastrophic consequences. Experts with experience applying AI and machine learning to cybersecurity infrastructure may be in high demand.

Combining AI cybersecurity with Blockchain technology would provide a more secure and decentralized approach in areas such as private data sharing, secure payment systems, and so on. This approach, which enhances the role of artificial intelligence in cyber security, has the potential to revolutionize the way digital assets are protected.

The prevalence of automated solutions makes it easier to mimic and augment human abilities, increase efficiency, and reduce the possibility of human error. According to Forbes, businesses are already investing billions of dollars in artificial intelligence (AI) and the industrial internet of things (IIoT) to implement intelligent technologies. The artificial intelligence market alone is expected to be worth $500 billion by 2025, according to this report.

The Future of Artificial Intelligence in Cyber Security market could grow at a compound annual growth rate of 24.2% from 2022 to 2029, reaching $66.22 billion.

The top three industries that use artificial intelligence are telecommunications, banking, and consumer goods. According to International Data Corporation, global cybersecurity spending may reach $174.7 billion by 2024.

Businesses must invest in advanced AI-integrated systems to remain competitive in the market and face evolving threats. According to a report, over 30,000 incidents of cybercrime were reported in 2019, with 4000 breaches resulting in data loss. In 2020, the average cost of a security breach to an organization was more than $8 million.

According to IBM, failure in early detection and combat causes severe losses, and the average cost of data breaches globally in 2022 was $4.35 million. Companies with fully implemented AI and automation programs saved $3.05 million.

The percentage of boards that see cybersecurity as a business risk has risen from 58% to 88% in the Gartner Board of Directors Survey 2022. As a result, the future of AI in cyber security may be a long road ahead.

Challenges Faced by Artificial Intelligence in Cybersecurity

Digital Transformation paves the way for growth, with a significant increase in the number of users active across multiple programs. AI's adaptability is a lethal weapon against security demons. In the meantime, technology has a long way to go to deal with artificial intelligence and cybersecurity opportunities and challenges.

With AI's enormous potential, outcomes from security channels appear to be improved with factors such as continuous learning and evolution, data handling, task elimination, self-updates, information analysis, and many more. And the future of AI in cyber security appears promising.

However, it also brings many challenges that cybersecurity may face, as the pulsating increase in intelligence does not stop at security. When considering the role of artificial intelligence in cyber security, opportunities to steal data do not fall through the cracks.

Affordability of Resources

The adoption of machine learning models and AI solutions necessitates the need for specialized equipment, infrastructure, and expertise to manage AI security systems. Given the significant financial investment required, not every medium or small-sized business, regardless of the potential threats they face, would be able to afford such costs. Furthermore, the expert market is smaller than global demand, which makes acquiring resources more difficult.

Dynamics of Economy

Things do not stop with the establishment of infrastructure, but also with the administration of IT systems. Artificial intelligence necessitates a high level of upkeep and management. Unless service providers offer AI security as a Software-as-a-Service (SaaS) or Platform-as-a-Service (PaaS) model, few businesses will be able to bear the costs and resources required to keep AI security systems operating at peak performance.

Half-Baked Internal Processes

Most businesses' security components are limited to tools and platforms, while improvements in internal processes and the need for cultural changes are overlooked due to capital investment restrictions. This demonstrates the failure of artificial intelligence-based security systems.

Following Data Privacy Laws

Machine learning is a subset of artificial intelligence, and given that AI improves over time, it is obvious that to train a security software system, a large amount of data and information would be required. While that is an obvious case, it may violate "right to be forgotten" laws. These systems handle massive amounts of data, and any discrepancy could result in unwanted theft.

Data Quality for Training

Machine learning is entirely dependent on the quality and effectiveness of the data used to train its algorithm. It is critical to either create a flexible yet robust data system for training or to draw real-time data from existing cybersecurity instances. Furthermore, to ensure the accuracy of results, classifiers and algorithm models must be evaluated from multiple perspectives. Creating a precise range of cybersecurity systems could be a daunting task that would require the assistance of experts in mathematics and artificial intelligence modeling from tech behemoths. This is the only way to assess the role of artificial intelligence in cyber security to its full potential.

Still, a non-negotiable requirement for teams to function

Regardless of the opportunities and challenges of artificial intelligence and cybersecurity, it is undeniable that AI cybersecurity programs embedded in company networks immunize internal defense systems to shorten prediction and detection times and prevent shortcoming breaches. Organizations can defeat malicious attacks by leveraging the power of AI. However, the intelligent system's decision-making power is dependent on its critical and creative thinking abilities, which require a lot more research. That means that machine learning cannot be completely relied on for some time.

Threat evolution is no longer a slow process, and as all of those processes of identifying and integrating solutions for distinct threats continue, more threats emerge in the public domain. The scope of implementation is broad. The security system could only detect and flag threats based on its learning. To improve precision, reinforced learning models are required. In the absence of this, AI systems may produce inaccurate results.

The implementation of AI cybersecurity solutions attracts a steady stream of data on a variety of factors and associated risks. Because more than half of cybersecurity breaches go unreported in the public domain, it makes it difficult for developers to collect data, compile it systematically for analysis, train the algorithms, and eventually create a robust AI security system.

Complex Encryptions to Data

Data encryption is undoubtedly a security measure from the user's perspective, but the use of advanced data encryption strategies makes it difficult for even the security system to eliminate any hidden threat. External packets are filtered using Deep Packet Inspection (DPI). However, the predefined code used to encrypt can also infiltrate the system as a predator.

Vulnerable to Attacks

Although they are security systems, AI cybersecurity can attract attacks. The regulations that cybersecurity tools are supposed to follow tend to be offensive to them. Manipulation and biases in an AI model's data can affect the machine learning language and input, resulting in incorrect decisions and breaches of confidential data privacy.

Can AI help us solve the world's most complex problems?

When we hear the word AI, the first images that come to mind are smart assistants building impressive gadgets at our command and terminator machines destroying the world.

However, in practice, AI is more positive and grounded. While AI has not yet reached the level of assembling gadgets, it has improved the world by solving many complex problems.

Online Shopping Made Easy

A few years ago, shopping for a product online without knowing its name was a nightmare. It took me hours to find that item in the catalog.

However, things are very different these days, thanks to AI trends such as predictive technology. When you search for something, even if you use a broad query, thousands of results appear in the blink of an eye.

We even get suggestions based on our searches, as if search engines could read our minds. Everything we desire appears to be within reach.

Companies like CamFind are taking this a step further by allowing you to identify objects by simply clicking on their image.

We are not far from the day when customers will be able to purchase ms simply by clicking on their image.

solved Faster and more precisely

The most difficult challenge for businesses is ensuring that their customers' questions are answered on time. Things become even more difficult when you are a large corporation with millions of customers.

HDFC, India's largest finance bank, was in the same boat. As a result, they created EVA (Electronic Virtual Assistant), an AI-based chatbot that collects knowledge from thousands of resources and provides simple answers in less than 0.4 seconds.

The virtual assistant has handled 3 million queries, interacted with half a million unique users, and held over half a million conversations.

So, you can see how much of an impact using AI in customer support can have.

Frauds Avoided

Tracing and preventing fraud have always been significant challenges, which AI is assisting us in overcoming. AI solutions are being used by organizations in a variety of industries to prevent fraud and improve security.

Companies such as MasterCard and RBSWordPay are using AI and deep learning to detect suspicious transaction patterns and prevent card fraud. Other industries are taking the same approach to avoid such scams. It has assisted them in saving millions of people from being duped out of their hard-earned money.

Farmers are growing more crops while using fewer resources.

According to statistics, we will need to produce 50% more food by 2050 due to our high consumption. Farmers will have to produce crops while using their resources wisely to achieve this.

Blue River Technology, a subsidiary of the American corporation John Deere, devised a solution in the form of a robot called See and Spray. The robot monitors and sprays weedicide on cotton plants in precise amounts using object detection (a computer vision technology).

Furthermore, PEAT, an agriculture startup, has developed Plantix, an app that uses image recognition technology to identify potential defects and provide techniques, tips, and solutions.

So, you can see how these minor details can help the agriculture industry and help us meet crop requirements.

We no longer have to be concerned about diseases.

You may have read this a hundred times before. But the only thing you can think of is "how is that possible?"

Cambio Health Care, a healthcare organization, has developed a clinical decision support system that alerts a physician when a patient is at risk of having a heart attack so that they can take appropriate precautions.

Another company, Coala Life, developed a digitalized device for detecting Cardiac diseases. Another company, Aifloo, is developing a system to monitor patients' health in nursing homes and healthcare facilities.

These examples demonstrate that we are not far from the day when we will no longer have to be concerned about finding a cure for new diseases. Instead, we can save more lives by utilizing existing cures.

E-learning is Much more Interactive & Fun Now

E-learning is one of the fastest-growing industries, with a market value of more than $325 billion expected by 2025. Keeping up with its pace, on the other hand, is a real challenge.

Millions of e-learning courses are available. How many do you believe to get the attention they deserve?

Fortunately, designing interactive courses is now simple thanks to artificial intelligence. AI is changing the face of e-learning with features such as learning pathways, personalized tutoring sessions, content analytics, targeted marketing, automatic grading, and real-time questioning.

It's no surprise that platforms such as Duolingo (30 million registered users) and Massive Open Online Courses (101 million registered users) are becoming increasingly popular.

Another interesting example of AI playing a critical role in eLearning that I recently discovered on the internet is an online PM training website. It creates interactive online training courses using AI and behavioral science.

As a result, AI is truly transforming the fate of eLearning and online education, making it more enjoyable and interactive.

Solving Puzzles is No Longer a Challenge

We all enjoy putting together puzzles. However, being stuck for hours trying to solve them is not something we would want.

For example, I am a Scrabble addict. It used to bother me, though, because I couldn't think of enough words. The most frustrating aspect was that I always lost when I played.

With the scrabble word finder, I recently discovered online, however, losing this game is out of the question because I can easily find the highest-scoring words.

Not only that, but AI is assisting historians in resolving ancient puzzles to restore and recreate historical artifacts from photos of fragments. Such things can make a significant contribution to humanity.

So, we're not far from the day when AI will solve every mystery and solve every puzzle. We are learning by playing games.

The majority of people will say no to this question.

However, thanks to artificial intelligence, this perception is about to change. AI is being used in games to train and improve players' skills.

AI is used to train players in the game F.E.A.R (First Encounter Assault Recon). The opponent AI's actions in this game are so unpredictable that it will train you to never make the same mistakes again. As the game becomes more difficult, you improve. It's no surprise that people like it.

Another fascinating example is Google DeepMind's AlphaZero, which is taking chess to the next level by defeating grandmasters such as Gary Kasparov and Vladimir Kramnik. The same thing is happening with AlphaGo.

So, thanks to artificial intelligence, games are teaching us to push our limits and improve in ways we never have before.

Combating Hate Speech and Trolls on social media Has Been Made Simple

Combating hate speech and trolls on social media has proven to be one of the most difficult challenges to date. Not only is it difficult to track down these trolls and hatemongers, but there is also little you can do about them. Twitter was having the same problem. As a result, it developed an AI that can easily identify hate speech and terrorist language using deep learning, machine learning, and natural language processing.

As a result, over 300,000 terrorist accounts have been blocked by the social media mogul. Even Facebook and Instagram have begun to employ AI to combat spammers, hatemongers, and trolls.

So, we are not far from the day when combating hate speech and trolls will no longer be a challenge.

Athletes Can Improve Their Performance

Being a sportsperson necessitates unwavering dedication and endless practice. However, practicing alone is not always sufficient. It must be combined with the appropriate strategy.

AI is assisting athletes in pushing their limits and achieving the impossible by breaking the game down into small chunks and then closely studying it with the help of machine learning algorithms.

Furthermore, the combination of sensor technology and AI is assisting coaches in improving players' techniques. It also aids in the prevention of player injuries by monitoring the levels of strain and exertion that players are subjected to.

All of these small details help players achieve impossible goals and elevate their performance to a whole new level.

In a Nutshell

While the concept of AI may still appear to be science fiction, it is already changing the world. These ten real-world examples demonstrate the point. It is assisting us in accomplishing what previously seemed impossible.

In the future, the trend will continue to revolutionize our lives. So, whether you are a beginner looking to start a career in AI or a business looking to incorporate the trend into your operations, now is the time.

Solving Global Problems

Machine learning and AI have the potential to extend beyond industries, providing assistance that can strengthen industries and economies as a whole. Consider the following SciPol examples:

Making driving safer

Though self-driving cars are still a few years away from being fully safe to drive, this area of AI has the potential to significantly reduce road deaths and injuries. According to a Stanford University report, self-driving cars have the potential to reduce traffic-related deaths and injuries. The change will also cause changes in our lifestyle, with passengers using the time saved from driving to get work done or entertain themselves on their commutes.

We may also have more flexibility in where we work as a result of self-driving cars, with the study reporting that increased comfort and decreased cognitive load may influence where people choose to live.

Transforming how we learn

The Georgia Tech News Center reported in 2016 that an artificial intelligence course resulted in the creation of an AI teaching assistant. Students enrolled in Georgia Tech's online Master of Science in Computer Science program discovered at the end of the course that their teaching assistant was a virtual assistant. And her work was necessary because the professor and his eight human TAs couldn't handle the workload with roughly 300 students enrolled and posting 10,000 messages in the online forums.

Following a few hiccups, the robot began answering the students' questions with 97% certainty. The university created the robot after discovering that one of the leading causes of student dropout was a lack of support. For universities, the use of this type of robot is revolutionary. People learn at different rates and different starting points. AI allows students to learn in a more personalized manner. And, because most educational systems cannot afford to tutor every child, AI can be used effectively.

Help us become more energy efficient

AI could help us be more efficient with our energy consumption, which is already happening in some parts of the world. Google's massive data center necessitates a massive amount of energy to run the servers and keep them cool. To counteract this effect, Google has used its AI platform Deep Mind to forecast when its data centers will become overheated. As a result, cooling systems are only activated when necessary, saving Google approximately 40% of its server farms.

Helping wildlife

The analysis of massive amounts of data allows for the transformation of wildlife. Tracking animal movements is one example of this, as it allows researchers to see where they go and, as a result, which habits need to be protected. For example, this Montana-based study identifies the best locations for wolverines and grizzly bears to establish wildlife corridors - continuous areas of protected land that connect zones of biological significance and allow animals to move safely through the wilderness.

Artificial intelligence programming

There are numerous programming languages used in the development of AI, each with its own set of advantages and disadvantages. Here are some of the most popular AI programming languages:

Python

Python is one of the most widely used programming languages in the field of artificial intelligence. It is a popular choice for AI applications due to its ease of use, readability, and extensive library support.

Python is a well-known high-level programming language that is used in a wide range of applications, including web development, scientific computing, data analysis, artificial intelligence, and machine learning. Guido van Rossum created it in the late 1980s intending to make it simple, easy to learn, and readable. Python has grown to be one of the most popular programming languages, with a large developer community contributing to its growth and development.

Python is known for its simple syntax and readability, making it an excellent language for beginning programmers. It is also extremely versatile, with numerous libraries and frameworks available for a variety of applications, including NumPy, Pandas, Scikit-learn, TensorFlow, Django, Flask, and many others.

Python is an interpreted language, which means that code can be run without being compiled. This facilitates the rapid development and testing of code, and it is widely used in the scientific community for data analysis and modeling. Python's dynamic typing and memory management also make it easier to write and maintain code, as well as develop and deploy applications faster.

Overall, Python is a powerful and adaptable programming language with applications ranging from web development to scientific computing and machine learning. It is widely regarded as one of the best programming languages for beginners to learn.

Python is one of the most widely used programming languages in artificial intelligence (AI). This is because Python has several features that make it ideal for developing AI applications.

Here are some of the ways Python is linked to AI:

Extensive Libraries

Python has some libraries designed specifically for AI development, including NumPy, Pandas, Scikit-learn, TensorFlow, Keras, and PyTorch. These libraries offer powerful data analysis, machine learning, deep learning, natural language processing, and computer vision tools.

Simple Syntax

Python's syntax is simple and readable, making it simple for developers to write and understand code, which is important in AI development where complex algorithms must be implemented.

Prototyping in a Hurry

Python's dynamic typing and ease of use make it an ideal language for rapid prototyping, allowing developers to build and test AI models in record time.

A sizable community

Python has a large and active developer community that has created many open-source AI development tools and libraries, making it easier for developers to get started with AI development and solve problems more efficiently.

Interoperability

Python is easily integrated with other programming languages, making it a versatile language that can be used alongside other tools and frameworks.

Python's extensive libraries, simple syntax, rapid prototyping capabilities, large community, and interoperability make it a natural fit for AI. Python is likely to remain a key language for AI development as AI evolves and becomes more important in various industries.

Python is a popular programming language for creating AI applications due to its simplicity, ease of use, and large developer community. Here are some examples of Python-based artificial intelligence projects:

Machine learning: Python has some popular machine learning libraries, such as Scikit-learn, TensorFlow, and PyTorch, which provide tools for developing and evaluating machine learning models. These libraries can be used for classification, regression, and clustering tasks.

Natural language processing: Python includes several powerful natural languages processing libraries, including NLTK, spaCy, and Gensim. These libraries can be used for sentiment analysis, topic modeling, and text classification, among other things.

Python is commonly used in the development of computer vision applications such as object detection, image segmentation, and facial recognition. OpenCV and DLib libraries provide powerful tools for image processing and computer vision tasks.

Python is widely used for data analysis and visualization, with libraries such as Pandas and Matplotlib offering data manipulation and graphing tools.

Python is frequently used for high-level control and scripting in robotics applications. For example, the Robot Operating System (ROS) includes Python APIs for developing robotics applications.

Python's ease of use, versatility and large developer community make it a popular choice for AI projects in a variety of industries, including e-commerce, finance, healthcare, and media. Its application in AI is most prevalent in machine learning, natural language processing, and computer vision.

Java

Another popular programming language used in AI development is Java, which is especially useful for creating large-scale enterprise applications. Because of its object-oriented programming structure and portability, it is a versatile choice for AI projects.

Sun Microsystems introduced Java, a popular high-level programming language, in 1995. It is platform-independent, which means that Java code can run on any computer or device with a Java Virtual Machine (JVM) installed, regardless of the underlying hardware or operating system.

Because Java is a statically typed language, variables must be declared with their data types before they can be used. It also supports object-oriented programming, which allows developers to create classes and objects to write code in a modular and reusable manner.

Memory management is one of Java's most important features. A garbage collector is used by Java to automatically free up memory that is no longer in use, which helps to prevent common memory management errors such as segmentation faults and memory leaks.

Java also has a rich set of libraries and frameworks that make complex application development easier, such as JavaFX for creating graphical user interfaces and Spring for creating web applications.

Overall, Java is a powerful and versatile programming language that is used in a wide range of applications, from web development to scientific computing to mobile app development.

Java can be used in a variety of ways in the development of artificial intelligence (AI). Here are a couple of examples:

Machine Learning: Java has some popular machine learning libraries, such as Weka and Deeplearning4j, that can be used to create and train machine learning models for a variety of tasks such as image recognition, natural language processing, and predictive analytics.

Natural Language Processing (NLP): Java includes a plethora of NLP APIs, such as the Stanford NLP library, OpenNLP, and Apache Lucene. These libraries enable the analysis and processing of human language data such as text and speech.

Robotics: Java can be used to create software for robotics applications such as robot control and sensor data analysis. The LeJOS (Java for Lego Mindstorms) project is a well-known example of how Java can be used in robotics development.

Java is frequently used in big data processing frameworks such as Apache Hadoop, Apache Spark, and Apache Flink. These frameworks are used for large dataset processing and complex data analytics tasks.

Java can also be used to create AI-based applications such as chatbots, recommendation systems, and fraud detection systems. Because of its rich libraries, robustness, and scalability, Java is an excellent choice for developing such applications.

C++

C++ is a high-performance programming language that is frequently used in the creation of artificial intelligence systems that require complex mathematical calculations or real-time processing.

Bjarne Stroustrup introduced C++, a popular high-level programming language, in 1983. It is an extension of the C programming language, and as such, it is sometimes referred to as "C with Classes". C++ is a general-purpose programming language that can be used for a wide range of applications such as system programming, embedded systems, game development, and more.

C++'s support for object-oriented programming is a key feature. By creating classes and objects, developers can write code in a modular and reusable manner. Other programming paradigms, such as procedural programming and generic programming, are also supported by C++.

C++ is a compiled language, which means that before it can be executed, the source code is compiled into machine code. This gives C++ programs an advantage over interpreted languages like Python or JavaScript in terms of performance.

C++ also allows for low-level access to the system's hardware and memory, making it a popular choice for creating operating systems, device drivers, and other low-level software.

C++ also has the following notable features:

Templates allow developers to write generic code that can be used with a variety of data types.

STL (Standard Template Library): The STL includes a set of container classes and algorithms for storing and manipulating data.

Handling Exceptions

C++ has a strong exception-handling mechanism that enables developers to handle errors and exceptions in a structured manner.

Overall, C++ is a strong and versatile programming language that is used in a wide range of applications. Because it supported OOP, low-level access, and performance benefits, it is a popular choice among many developers.

C++ can be used in a variety of ways in the development of artificial intelligence (AI). Here are a couple of examples:

Learning Machines

Because of its speed and low-level memory access, C++ is a popular language for developing high-performance machine learning algorithms. TensorFlow, Caffe, and Torch all have C++ APIs and can be used to create machine-learning models.

Because of its ability to efficiently process large amounts of image and video data, Computer Vision C++ is a popular choice for developing computer vision algorithms. OpenCV is a popular computer vision library with a C++ interface that is widely used in the artificial intelligence community.

C++ is a popular programming language for robotics development, particularly for low-level control systems. ROS (Robot Operating System) is a popular open-source robotics framework with a C++ API.

C++ can be used to develop high-performance Natural Language Processing (NLP) applications that require efficient memory management and low-level control. The Stanford NLP library, which has a C++ interface, can be used to create NLP applications.

Optimization

Algorithms for optimization problems such as linear programming, quadratic programming, and mixed-integer programming can be written in C++. C++ APIs are available for libraries such as CPLEX, Gurobi, and MOSEK, which can be used to develop optimization models.

C++'s overall performance and low-level control make it a popular choice for developing AI applications requiring high-performance computation, efficient memory management, and low-level access to the system's hardware.

Here are some examples of C++-based artificial intelligence projects:

Vision in computers

C++ is commonly used in the development of computer vision applications such as object detection, image segmentation, and facial recognition. OpenCV and DLib libraries provide powerful tools for image processing and computer vision tasks.

Vehicles that drive themselves

C++ is widely used in the development of software for autonomous vehicles such as self-driving cars and drones. C++ can be used for real-time control and decision-making algorithms, as well as sensor and hardware interfacing.

Robotics

For real-time control and performance-critical algorithms, C++ is frequently used in robotics applications. C++ can be used to build algorithms for path planning, motion control, and machine vision, as well as to interface with sensors and motors.

Natural language processing

C++ has been used in a variety of natural language processing (NLP) applications, most notably speech recognition and synthesis. For example, the Kaldi toolkit uses C++ to build speech recognition systems.

AI in gaming

In game development, C++ is frequently used to create AI agents that can learn and adapt to player behavior. The Open AI Five system, for example, which plays the game Dota 2, was created using C++ and other programming languages.

Overall, C++ is a versatile programming language that is well-suited for AI applications requiring speed, efficiency, and low-level hardware control. Its application in AI is most common in computer vision, robotics, and autonomous systems.

R

R is a programming language that was created specifically for statistical analysis and data visualization, making it a popular choice for AI applications with large datasets.

R is a statistical computing, data analysis, and graphics programming language and environment. It was created in 1993 at the University of Auckland, New Zealand, by Ross Ihaka and Robert Gentleman, and is now maintained by the R Development Core Team.

R includes a wide range of statistical and graphical techniques, such as linear and nonlinear modeling, time series analysis, clustering, and traditional statistical tests. It also comes with several graphical tools for data visualization and exploration. Furthermore, R has a robust user-contributed package system that allows access to additional functionality.

R is a free and open-source data analysis and statistical computing software that is distributed under the GNU General Public License. It is widely used in academia, industry, and government agencies. It has a large and active user and developer community that contributes to the development of new packages and extensions as well as provides support and resources via online forums, mailing lists, and user groups. R is also integrated with other programming languages and tools, such as Python and SQL, making it simple for users to incorporate R into their existing workflows.

R's key features include the following:

Data management

R includes several data structures for efficient data manipulation and analysis, including vectors, matrices, arrays, data frames, and lists.

Graphics

R includes a robust graphics system for data visualization and exploration, as well as a variety of 2D and 3D plotting functions.

R is a complete programming language that supports functions, loops, conditional statements, and other programming constructs.

Data analysis

R includes a comprehensive set of data analysis and modeling tools, such as linear and nonlinear regression, clustering, classification, and time-series analysis.

R is a powerful and flexible statistical computing and data analysis language with a large and active user and developer community.

The R programming language is widely used in the field of AI because of its statistical and data analysis capabilities (Artificial Intelligence). R is commonly used to create predictive models, machine learning algorithms, and deep learning models.

R includes some statistical functions and packages that are commonly used in AI applications. The 'caret' package, for example, provides a comprehensive framework for developing and comparing machine learning models, whereas the 'neuralnet' package provides tools for developing neural network models. R also includes many packages for natural language processing, image recognition, and other artificial intelligence-related tasks.

Furthermore, R is frequently used in tandem with other AI-related tools and languages, such as Python and TensorFlow. R can be used to perform data preprocessing and statistical analysis, whereas Python and TensorFlow can be used to build and train machine learning models.

R's strong statistical capabilities make it a popular choice for data analysis and modeling in the field of AI, and it is frequently used in AI workflows alongside other tools and languages.

The R programming language has been used in several AI projects. Here are a few examples:

Recommender systems

In the e-commerce and media industries, recommender systems are commonly used to suggest items to users based on their preferences and behavior. R includes several packages, such as recommended and surprise,' that provide tools for developing and evaluating recommender systems.

Natural language processing

Several packages in R, such as 'tm,' 'openNLopen NLP,' and 'quanteda,' provide tools for processing and analyzing text data. These tools are useful for tasks like sentiment analysis, topic modeling, and text classification.

Image analysis

R includes several packages, including 'imager' and 'EBImage,' that provide tools for image processing and analysis. These software packages can be used for image segmentation, object recognition, and image classification.

Machine learning

Several R packages, such as 'caret,' 'randomForest,' and 'glmnet,' provide tools for developing and evaluating machine learning models. These packages can be used to perform classification, regression, and clustering tasks.

Time series analysis

z-+R has several packages for analyzing time series data, including 'forecast' and 'xts'. These packages are useful for forecasting, anomaly detection, and trend analysis.

R is a popular choice for AI projects in a variety of fields, including e-commerce, finance, healthcare, and media, due to its flexibility and comprehensive set of packages.

Lisp

Lisp is an older programming language that has been extensively used in the development of artificial intelligence systems. It is well-suited for certain types of AI applications due to its ability to handle symbolic reasoning and dynamic memory allocation.

LISP is a programming language that was developed in the late 1950s and is still in use today. LISP is frequently associated with AI because it was one of the first programming languages used in AI research.

LISP's support for symbolic programming is one of the main reasons it is well-suited for AI. Programs in LISP can manipulate symbols and expressions as data, allowing the development of complex knowledge representation systems, expert systems, and other AI applications.

LISP has written several AI projects, some of which are shown below:

Expert systems

LISP was widely used in the development of expert systems, which are computer programs that simulate the decision-making ability of a human expert in a particular domain. CLIPS (C Language Integrated Production System), the expert system shell, is written in LISP.

Natural language processing

LISP has been used in some natural language processing (NLP) applications, most notably in the development of knowledge representation systems capable of reasoning about language. For example, the Cyc project is a large-scale knowledge representation system written in LISP.

Robotics

LISP has been used in some robotics applications, most notably in the development of high-level control systems. The NASA Mars Rover, for example, was controlled by the Rover Sequencing and Visualization Program, a LISP-based system (RSVP).

Machine learning

LISP has been used in the development of rule-based systems and decision trees in some machine-learning applications. For example, the ID3 algorithm, which is used for decision tree learning, was originally written in LISP.

While LISP is no longer as widely used in AI as it once was, it still has a place in the field and has made significant contributions to the advancement of AI over the years. Its application in AI is most common in expert systems, natural language processing, and robotics.

Prolog

Prolog is a programming language that is frequently used in the creation of expert systems and other types of AI applications involving logical reasoning.

Overall, the programming language used for AI development will be determined by the project's specific requirements as well as the developer's or development team's preferences.

Prolog (Programming in Logic) is a logic-based programming language that is widely used in artificial intelligence. PROLOG is especially well-suited for applications requiring complex relationship and rule reasoning.

Following are some examples of AI projects written in Prolog:

Expert systems

Prolog is frequently used in the development of expert systems, which are computer programs that simulate the decision-making ability of a human expert in a specific domain. Expert systems are typically built in Prolog using a set of rules and facts that describe the domain.

Natural language processing

Prolog has been used in some natural language processing (NLP) applications, most notably in the development of systems capable of parsing and reasoning about natural language statements. For example, the Natural Language Understanding System (NLU) is a Prolog-based system that can understand English sentences.

Semantic web

Prolog has been used in the development of the semantic web, a World Wide Web extension aimed at making data more easily shareable and understandable by computers. Ontologies, which are typically built with PROLOG, are used to represent data in the semantic web.

Game AI

Prolog has been used in some game AI applications, most notably in the creation of expert systems for gameplay. For example, the General Game Playing system is a Prolog-based system that can play a wide range of games.

Prolog's emphasis on logic and reasoning makes it ideal for AI applications requiring complex rule-based systems. Its application in AI is most common in expert systems, natural language processing, the semantic web, and game AI.

References

1. Artificial Intelligence: A Modern Approach by Stuart Russell and Peter Norvig
2. Human Compatible: Artificial Intelligence and the Problem of Control by Stuart Russell
3. Superintelligence: Paths, Dangers, Strategies by Nick Bostrom
4. The Hundred-Page Machine Learning Book by Andriy Burkov
5. Artificial Intelligence: A Modern Approach by Stuart Russell and Peter Norvig
6. Deep Learning by Ian Goodfellow, Yoshua Bengio, and Aaron Courville
7. Race After Technology: Abolitionist Tools for the New Jim Code by Ruha Benjamin
8. Weapons of Math Destruction: How Big Data Increases Inequality and Threatens Democracy by Cathy O'Neil
9. Artificial Intelligence: A Modern Approach by Stuart Russell and Peter Norvig
10. Deep Learning" by Ian Goodfellow, Yoshua Bengio, and Aaron Courville
11. Machine Learning: A Probabilistic Perspective by Kevin Murphy
12. Hands-On Machine Learning with Scikit-Learn, Keras, and TensorFlow by Aurélien Géron
13. Deep Learning in Medical Image Analysis by S. Kevin Zhou, Hayit Greenspan, and Dinggang Shen
14. Medical Image Analysis with Deep Learning by Le Lu, Yefeng Zheng, Gustavo Carneiro, and Lin Yang
15. Jobs Lost, Jobs Gained: What the Future of Work Will Mean for Jobs, Skills, and Wages by James Manyika, Susan Lund, Michael Chui, Jacques Bughin, Jonathan Woetzel, Parul Batra, Ryan Ko, and Saurabh Sanghvi.
16. Global Demographics: A New Business Frontier by Richard Dobbs, Sven Smit, and Fabian Schaer.

17. Globalization, Women, and Work by Stephanie Seguino and Mark Setterfield.
18. Artificial Intelligence: A Modern Approach by Stuart Russell and Peter Norvig.
19. Programming Game AI by Example by Mat Buckland.

www.ingramcontent.com/pod-product-compliance
Lightning Source LLC
La Vergne TN
LVHW010101110826
845155LV00028B/436

* 9 7 8 1 9 4 7 4 6 4 4 0 7 *